The Soy
Sauce
Cookbook

The Soy Sauce Cookbook

Explore the flavor-enhancing power of the Orient's magic ingredient.

Jenny Stacey and Maureen Keller

CHARTWELL
BOOKS, INC.

A QUINTET BOOK

Published by Chartwell Books
A Division of Book Sales, Inc.
114 Northfield Avenue
Edison, New Jersey 08837

This edition produced for sale in the U.S.A., its
territories and dependencies only.

ISBN 0-7858-0659-8

This book was designed and produced by
Quintet Publishing Limited
6 Blundell Street
London N7 9BH

Creative Director: Richard Dewing
Designer: James Lawrence
Art Director: Patrick Carpenter
Project Editors: Katie Preston and Kathy Steer
Editor: Barbara Croxford
Photographer: David Armstrong
Home Economist: Gina Steer

Typeset in Great Britain by
Central Southern Typesetters, Eastbourne
Manufactured in Malaysia by
C. H. Colourscan Sdn Bhd
Printed in Singapore by
Star Standard Industries Pte Ltd

Photographs on pages 7, 8 (tr), 9, 10, 11
courtesy of Kikkoman Soy Sauce

Contents

Introduction

Known as Shoyu or "fermented savory agent" in Japan and jiang yong in China, soy sauce is as indispensable to cooks and chefs in China and Japan as salt, pepper, and mustard are elsewhere. It is an essential component of Chinese and Asian cooking. Every table hosts a bottle of soy sauce at all mealtimes to be used as a seasoning or dip.

We still associate soy sauce with Asian recipes and cooking methods, and do not use it to its full potential. In fact, soy sauce is a versatile performer that can be used as a basis for rich sauces, broths, dips, marinades, or simply drizzled over roast or fried dishes, enhancing everything it touches with its uniquely piquant flavor.

Barbecued Fish Steaks ▲

Dark soy sauce is matured for a longer period than light soy, and so it attains its dark, almost black appearance. Slightly thicker than light soy, it has a stronger, sweeter flavor and is more suitable for stews, casseroles, and recipes with dark meats. It is also the sauce used where a dipping sauce consisting only of soy sauce is called for. It is known in Chinese grocers as Soy Superior Sauce. The two names are very similar, and care should be taken not to confuse them.

Lamb with Cranberry Sauce ▲

Japanese Soy Sauce production drawing ▶

There are two main types of soy sauce, the light and the dark varieties. These again are very distinctive, each blending best with different foods.

Light soy sauce, as the name implies, is light in color and less powerful in flavor, although the flavor remains full. It is the most widely used for the sauces, being the most suitable for use in cooking. Saltier than dark soy sauce, it is known in Chinese super-markets as Superior Soy and is mainly used in soups and with fish, seafood and light meats, and poultry.

What is Soy Sauce?

Called liquid spice, naturally brewed soy sauce contains more than 280 aromatic ingredients including extract of vanilla, fruits, flowers, meat, fish, and alcohol which enable it to enhance many dishes with its subtle bouquet. Based on soy beans, wheat, water, salt, and a specially developed yeast, soy sauce is brewed in a similar fashion to a fine wine. Other ingredients are added according to the origin of the sauce. Pork is added in Canton, ginger and mushrooms in Peking, and occasionally anchovy paste. Naturally brewed soy sauce is free from additives and preservatives. There are, however, other less natural processes which chemically produce soy sauce. These are considered to be inferior in aroma and flavor by true soy sauce connoisseurs.

The History of Soy Sauce

Japanese soy sauce was first introduced to the West by Dutch explorers in the 17th century. It was they who introduced it to Europe, exporting it in stone jars and barrels. Soy sauce soon became popular in France, where the royal chefs of Louis XIV discovered its uses as a flavor enhancer.

The Chinese, however, were the original users of soy sauce. They introduced it to Japan, along with the influence of Buddhism, over 1,500 years ago. The Buddhist religion forbade the use of meat and fish-based sauces, which traditionally played a great part in flavoring foods. Soy sauce soon became a popular seasoning in Japan although it was developed and changed from its original form: it was originally made only from soy beans, and the Japanese version had wheat added to it. The piquant sauce has of course now progressed even further to its present fine form, there being various methods of production and a wide selection of sauces on the market.

◀ *TOP LEFT: Light Soy Sauce*

TOP RIGHT: A traditional Soy Sauce ceramic jar

BOTTOM LEFT: A modern collection of Soy Sauce bottles

BOTTOM RIGHT: Dark Soy Sauce

How Soy Sauce is Produced

Very simply, naturally brewed soy sauce is produced when soy beans and wheat are mixed together to form a "starter" known as "koji". The koji mixture grows over a period of 45 hours, during which time special enzymes vital to the final flavor, color, and aroma of the sauce begin to form. Next, a salt water solution is added and the mixture is left to ferment for up to six months. The resulting mixture is known as a "mature mash" and resembles a smooth, reddish brown liquid. The mash is then pressed between layers of cloth and the clear soy sauce is extracted. This is then pasteurized and bottled.

There are 280 different flavor and aroma components to a good soy sauce. They blend in such a way that no one particular flavor is dominant,

The Imperial Soy Sauce Museum, Goyogura ▲

resulting in a product that may be used with a wide variety of ingredients. Some soy sauces are now made from hydrolyzed vegetable protein with the addition of corn syrup, caramel, and other artificial substances. The resulting flavor of this type of sauce is far less pleasant than naturally brewed soy sauce and it is well worth trying to purchase the latter.

There are three methods of producing soy sauce, and the end products vary in quality and flavor:

This fermented or brewed soy sauce is produced by fermenting soy beans, wheat, water, and salt with no further additions.

This type of non-brewed sauce is chemically produced by hydrolyzing plant protein, which is then blended with colorings, salt water, corn syrup, and caramel.

This soy sauce combined or semi-brewed soy sauce is produced by combining the two previous methods together.

Artificial or chemically produced soy sauce is made when the vegetable or plant proteins are decomposed at a high temperature by the addition of powerful acids such as hydrochloric acid. This mixture is then neutralized with the addition of soda. The final

Soy fermenting in chrysanthemum wood vats ▼

Ancient Japanese Soy Sauce production drawing ▶

10

additions are HVP, sugar, salt, and caramel. The final product is considered to be lacking in flavor and aroma when compared to naturally brewed soy sauce, such as Japanese brands.

Chinese-style soy sauce is different again. This ferments in just 30 days. The lack of yeast gives a fermentation low in alcohol and lactic acids and a resultant sauce which some say lacks flavor and aroma.

Japanese naturally brewed soy sauce is made by traditional methods that have been handed down for 350 years. First, soy beans are steamed and then mixed with kernels of roasted, crushed wheat in equal proportions. Yeast is then added to start the natural fermentation process. After three days, the soy and wheatgerm mixture grows a mold over the surface, at which stage it is known as "koji", as mentioned on page 9. The mixture is now blended with salted water and the resultant wet mash put into fermentation tanks.

Over a period of weeks, the soy bean protein changes to amino acids, which give that characteristic taste to the final sauce. Wheat starch changes to sugar and the mixture of this and the acids forms the color of the sauce. The sugar content gradually changes to alcohol and some of the alcohol and sugar transforms into various acids which add tartness to the flavor. This mixture matures for six months and is then pressed. The liquid, which is the soy sauce, is drawn off, pasteurized, and bottled.

Soy Sauce Today

You can see from these different processes that there are different qualities of soy sauce on the market today. If possible, try to use the naturally brewed sauces in your cooking for full flavor.

There is an ancient taste test which is said to distinguish between a good sauce and a lesser sauce. A good sauce can be enjoyed neat if poured into a small dish. A lesser sauce would be too harsh and unpleasant if taken in this way.

Soy sauce was initially used as a seasoning by the Chinese to complement their vegetarian diet; now, it is also used in stewed dishes and marinades in China and in Indonesia as a table condiment. It may be used in many types of cooking, not all of them Asian, and with many ingredients. The addition of soy sauce gives a unique spicy, salty flavor to dishes without overpowering it. Soy sauce is generally used in small quantities, as you will see from the following array of recipes. Another advantage of soy sauce as a condiment and flavor-enhancer is that it has an indefinite shelf life if stored correctly, and so does not need to be used quickly. Store the sauce as you would a fine wine, with its cap firmly sealed, and keep it in the refrigerator or a cool place to prevent it from oxidizing. Once you begin to realize the full potential of soy sauce by trying the delicious recipes featured in the pages that follow, long storage will not be an issue you have to consider. So get out that bottle of soy sauce and enter a world of new tastes in the kitchen.

CHAPTER ONE

Adventurous Appetizers

Stuffed Mushrooms

Capers, feta cheese, and soy sauce give these stuffed mushrooms a taste of the Middle East.

MAKES 14 TO 16 MUSHROOMS

¾ **lb large mushrooms (14 to 16)**

¼ **cup crumbled feta cheese**

¼ **cup Italian-style bread crumbs**

½ **tsp. olive oil (plus additional oil for brushing the mushrooms)**

1 **tsp. light soy sauce**

½ **tsp. ground thyme**

1 **tsp. grated onion**

3 **tsp. capers, drained**

● Wash the mushrooms and remove the stems. Chop the stems very finely and place in a bowl. Add 3 tablespoons of the cheese, the bread crumbs and mix thoroughly. Stir in the olive oil and soy sauce. When well blended, stir in the thyme, grated onion, and drained capers.

● Brush the mushroom caps with olive oil, inside and out. Stuff with the bread crumb mixture. Then crumble the remaining tablespoon of feta over the mushrooms. Broil until heated thoroughly and tops begin to brown, 6–8 minutes.

Marinated Mushroom Caps

These tasty mushrooms get better the longer they marinate. They are delicious whole, but also can be sliced and added to liven up salads.

SERVES 6

2 cups fresh white mushrooms

2 Tbsp. light soy sauce

¼ cup red wine (Merlot is recommended)

2 Tbsp. red wine vinegar

1 Tbsp. sugar

● Remove and discard stems from the mushrooms. Wash the caps and pat them dry. Place the caps in a bowl or jar with a tight lid. Mix together the soy sauce, wine, vinegar, and sugar. Pour over the mushroom caps.

● Marinate the mushrooms in the refrigerator at least overnight or up to three days, turning occasionally. Serve in a bowl with toothpicks.

Pork Spareribs

Traditionally quite a time-consuming dish, these ribs are cut into smaller pieces and cooked in a wok. They do not require marinating because they are cooked in a spicy barbecue sauce.

SERVES 4

1½ lb country-style pork ribs, cut into 2 inch pieces

2 Tbsp. vegetable oil

3 Tbsp. dark soy sauce

3 Tbsp. honey

2 Tbsp. Worcestershire sauce

⅔ cup strained tomatoes

1 tsp. ground ginger

2 garlic cloves, minced

¼ tsp. Chinese five spice powder

3 Tbsp. red wine vinegar

3 oz soft dark brown sugar

2 Tbsp. lime juice

● Prepare the ribs and heat the oil in a wok. Add the ribs and cook until brown, 5 minutes. Reduce heat and cook a further 10 minutes.

● Place all the remaining ingredients in a saucepan and heat gently to dissolve the sugar.

● Pour the sauce into the wok with the ribs. Cover and cook until the ribs are well cooked through, about 30 minutes. Serve.

Salmon Pâté ▲

Salmon Pâté

This is a really speedy, yet delicious appetizer. Once the fish is cooked, all the ingredients are simply blended in a food processor. For extra speed, use canned salmon.

● Poach the salmon fillets in a large shallow pan 8–10 minutes or until cooked through. Remove from the pan, drain, and skin the fish. Chop the fish into pieces and let cool completely.

● Place the cream cheese, soy sauce, dill, parsley, lemon juice, capers, pepper, and cooked salmon in a food processor and blend 15 seconds.

● Transfer to four individual serving dishes. Sprinkle with paprika and chill until required. Garnish and serve with hot toast triangles.

S E R V E S   4

8 oz salmon fillet

½ cup cream cheese

1 Tbsp. light soy sauce

1 Tbsp. chopped fresh dill

1 Tbsp. chopped fresh parsley

1 Tbsp. lemon juice

1 Tbsp. capers

ground black pepper

½ tsp. paprika

dill sprigs and lemon slices

Garbanzo Bean Soup

A variation on a Greek recipe, this colorful garbanzo bean and tomato soup is quite filling. The soy sauce brings out the true flavors of this delicious appetizer.

SERVES 4

1½ cups dried garbanzo beans, soaked overnight, rinsed and drained

6¼ cups vegetable stock

3 Tbsp. olive oil

2 red onions, halved and sliced

2 celery stalks, chopped

3 garlic cloves, minced

3 Tbsp. tomato paste

2 tomatoes, skinned, seeded, and diced

2 Tbsp. chopped fresh cilantro

2 Tbsp. lemon juice

2 Tbsp. light soy sauce

chopped fresh cilantro

● Place the garbanzo beans in a large pan, cover with water, and bring to a boil. Boil rapidly 15 minutes, then drain and rinse well, discarding the cooking liquor.

● Return the garbanzo beans to the pan and pour in the vegetable stock. Return to a boil. Skim off any foam with a draining spoon, cover, and simmer until the beans are tender, 1½–1¾ hours.

● Meanwhile, heat the oil in a skillet and sauté the onions, celery, and garlic 5 minutes, stirring. Add the tomato paste and tomatoes and cook 3–4 minutes. Stir into the garbanzo beans.

● Transfer the soup to a blender and purée 15 seconds. Return to the pan and add the cilantro, lemon juice, and soy sauce. Sprinkle with cilantro and serve with warm crusty bread.

Hot and Sour Shrimp Soup

This really is a colorful soup in all aspects. Filled with shrimp and vegetables, it has a truly unique flavor.

SERVES 4

4 dried Chinese mushrooms

3¾ cups vegetable stock

1 cup peeled cooked shrimp

¾ cup sliced pickled Chinese vegetables

½ cup canned bamboo shoots, drained and sliced

3 scallions, sliced

1 zucchini, shredded

½-inch piece fresh ginger root, shredded

2 tomatoes, seeded and diced

2 tsp. rice wine or sherry

2 Tbsp. light soy sauce

1 Tbsp. red wine vinegar

2 Tbsp. diced smoked ham

1 tsp. sesame oil

● Soak the dried mushrooms in warm water for 20 minutes. Squeeze dry, remove the stems, and slice.

● In a large saucepan, bring the stock to a boil. Add the shrimp, vegetables, bamboo shoots, scallions, zucchini, ginger, and tomatoes. Simmer 5 minutes.

● Add the rice wine or sherry, soy sauce, vinegar, and ham. Cook 1 minute and stir in the sesame oil. Serve immediately.

18

Curried Parcels

Easy to prepare, these parcels may be served hot or cold, perhaps with a mint and yogurt dip to complement the Indian flavors in the filling.

SERVES 4

3 oz prepared puff pastry, thawed

1 egg, beaten

1 tsp. sesame seeds

For the Filling

1 Tbsp. butter

2 scallions, chopped

2 garlic cloves, minced

1 tsp. garam masala

½ tsp. chile powder

1 Tbsp. peach chutney

2 tsp. lemon juice

1 small carrot, finely diced

1 Tbsp. light soy sauce

¾ cup diced cooked potato

● Melt the butter for the filling and gently cook the scallions, garlic, garam masala, chile, chutney, lemon juice, carrot, and soy sauce, stirring, 3–4 minutes. Add the potato, mix well, and let cool completely.

● Heat the oven to 400°F. Roll out the pastry into a 8-inch square. Cut into four 4-inch squares. Brush the edges of the squares with beaten egg and place a little filling in the center of each square. Carefully draw the corners to the center to form a parcel, sealing the seams by pressing gently together. Repeat with all of the squares.

● Place the parcels on a dampened baking sheet, brush with beaten egg, and sprinkle with the sesame seeds. Bake in the oven until risen and golden, about 15 minutes.

Country Pâté

This pâté is lighter than most meat pâtés, being made with chicken and pork. The marinating of the meat lets it fully absorb all the different flavors.

SERVES 8

1¼ cups minced chicken breast

1 cup minced fresh pork slices

⅔ cup finely diced smoked bacon

½ tsp. salt

½ tsp. ground nutmeg

2 garlic cloves, minced

1 tsp. cumin seeds

2 tsp. mixed peppercorns

5 Tbsp. brandy

2 Tbsp. light soy sauce

● Lightly grease a 2 lb loaf pan. Place the chicken, pork, and bacon in a large mixing bowl. Add the salt, nutmeg, garlic, and cumin. Crush the peppercorns and add to the mixture with the brandy and soy sauce. Mix very well, cover, and let sit at least 1 hour.

● Heat the oven to 300°F. Spoon the mixture into the loaf pan, pressing down well. Place in a roasting pan half filled with hot water. Cook the pâté in the oven until cooked through, 1½–1¾ hours. Remove from the water and let cool completely. Unmold the pâté, slice, and serve with hot toast or bread.

Spicy Peanuts

Plain peanuts make a good appetizer, but spicy peanuts are even better. Use a hot curry powder and serve them with lots of beer.

MAKES 1 LB

1 Tbsp. olive oil

2 large garlic cloves, minced

1 lb roasted, unsalted peanuts

1 Tbsp. light soy sauce

1 Tbsp. Worcestershire sauce

1 tsp. curry powder

● Heat the oil in a pan and add the garlic, stirring. Add the peanuts, soy sauce, Worcestershire sauce, and curry powder. Sauté a few minutes until the liquid has been absorbed. Remove from the heat and cool.

22

Hot and Spicy Chicken Wings

A real favorite for supper, these chicken wings are also perfect for barbecues. Try using boned chicken thighs or drumsticks if wings are not readily available.

SERVES 4

2 lb chicken wings

2 Tbsp. garlic wine vinegar

2 Tbsp. honey

1 Tbsp. Worcestershire sauce

2 Tbsp. dark soy sauce

a few drops of Tabasco sauce

1 Tbsp. tomato paste

⅔ cup strained tomatoes

1 tsp. prepared mustard

● Heat the oven to 350°F. Place the chicken wings in a shallow ovenproof dish.

● Place the vinegar, honey, Worcestershire sauce, soy sauce, Tabasco sauce, tomato paste, strained tomatoes, and mustard in a bowl. Mix well. Pour over the chicken wings, turning to coat well.

● Cook the chicken wings in the oven until cooked through, 45 minutes. Serve hot with salad.

Hawaiian Meatballs

Mangos and coconut make these meatballs a treat at any cocktail party. Keep them warm in a chafing dish and serve with toothpicks.

● Preheat the oven to 350°F. Chop the mango chutney and place in a mixing bowl. Add the ground beef, coconut, onion, nutmeg, parsley, garlic, and soy sauce. Season with pepper.

● Bring the mixture together with your hands, mixing well and roll into 24 equal sized balls. Place on an ungreased baking sheet. Cook in the oven until browned and cooked through, about 30 minutes. Serve hot.

MAKES 24

about ½ cup mango chutney

2 cups ground beef round

⅔ cup shredded coconut

1 onion, finely chopped

dash of ground nutmeg

1 Tbsp. chopped fresh parsley

1 garlic clove, minced

1 Tbsp. dark soy sauce

ground black pepper

Fried Shrimp Rolls

Asian in flavor, these shrimp-filled bites are delicious, with a hint of coconut and lime to complement the fish. Prepare in advance and store in the refrigerator for cooking just before serving.

● Using a rolling pin, flatten the bread slices until very thin. Melt the butter in a pan, add the flour, and mix well. Cook 1 minute, then add the coconut milk and bring to a boil, stirring. Remove the pan from the heat and stir in the soy sauce, cheese, lime rind, shrimp, and scallions. Season with pepper.

● Spread the mixture onto the bread, roll up, and cut each slice into four. Mix the dip ingredients and chill until required.

● Heat the oil for frying to 370°F. Meanwhile, in a bowl mix together the bread crumbs and sesame seeds. Place the beaten egg in a separate bowl. Dip each piece into the egg and then roll in the crumb mixture to coat completely. Fry in the hot oil 3 minutes. Drain on paper towels and serve with the dip.

SERVES 4

4 thick slices white bread, with crusts removed

1 Tbsp. butter, softened

1 Tbsp. all-purpose flour

2 Tbsp. coconut milk

1 Tbsp. light soy sauce

1 Tbsp. Romano cheese, shredded

grated rind of 1 lime

½ cup peeled cooked shrimp, chopped

2 scallions, finely chopped

ground black pepper

oil for deep frying

1 egg, beaten

1 cup fresh brown bread crumbs

1 Tbsp. sesame seeds

For the Dip

⅔ cup yogurt

⅔ cup mayonnaise

1 tsp. fish sauce

1 Tbsp. tomato paste

1 tsp. lime juice

1 Tbsp. chopped fresh parsley

Sesame Pikelets ▲

Sesame Pikelets

Pikelets are a form of traditional pancake. The batter, unlike others, should be made just before cooking. It is thicker than a pancake batter in order to hold its shape in the pan.

● Sieve the flour into a large mixing bowl. Add the sesame seeds and make a well in the center, gradually whisking in the butter, milk, and soy sauce.

● Grease a large heavy based skillet with butter. Drop 2 tablespoons of mixture into the skillet for each pikelet, cooking two at a time. Cook until the surface of the pikelet bubbles, turn to brown the other side for 2–3 minutes. Cool on a rack. Repeat until all the mixture is used.

● Slice the trout fillets. Mix half of the herbs into the sour cream. Spoon the sour cream onto the pikelets, top with the trout and sprinkle on remaining herbs. Serve with a small salad.

SERVES 4

For the Pikelets

1 cup self-rising flour

1 tsp. sesame seeds

2 Tbsp. butter, melted

⅔ cup milk

1 Tbsp. light soy sauce

For the Topping

8 oz smoked trout fillets

2 Tbsp. snipped fresh chives

1 Tbsp. chopped fresh dill

⅔ cup sour cream

lemon wedges

Vegetable Beignets

Crisp vegetables fried in a light batter, which lets the true colors of the vegetables be seen, make an attractive and delicious appetizer when served with the spicy tomato sauce.

SERVES 4

¾ lb mixed vegetables, such as asparagus spears, peppers, snow peas, cauliflower, and broccoli

oil for deep frying

For the Batter

1 egg

⅔ cup water

1 Tbsp. light soy sauce

1 cup all-purpose flour

½ cup cornstarch

dash of salt

For the Sauce

1 red chile, chopped

4 Tbsp. light soy sauce

4 Tbsp. vermouth

⅓ cup strained tomatoes

¼ cup vegetable stock

1 Tbsp. soft brown sugar

● Blanch the vegetables 3 minutes, drain well, and pat dry with paper towels. Mix together the sauce ingredients. Place in a small pan and heat gently until the sugar dissolves. Keep warm.

● Beat the egg, water, and soy sauce for the batter. Sieve the flour, cornstarch, and salt into a bowl. Make a well in the center and gradually whisk in the egg mixture to form a smooth batter.

● Heat the oil to 370°F in a wok. Dip the vegetables into the batter, then deep fry in the oil 2–3 minutes. Remove with a slotted spoon and drain on paper towels. Serve with the dipping sauce.

CHAPTER TWO

Piquant Poultry Dishes

Chicken in Black Bean Sauce

This sauce is very easy to make and far superior to the bottled sauce you can buy. If you have dried black beans, prepare them in the usual way and then use as canned beans in the recipe.

SERVES 4

1 cup vegetable oil

12 oz boned chicken breast, cut into strips

1 cup oyster mushrooms

1 small yellow bell pepper, diced

1 small green bell pepper, diced

6 scallions, chopped

½ cup snow peas

2 Tbsp. canned black beans, washed

½ inch piece fresh ginger root, shredded

1 garlic clove, minced

2 Tbsp. sherry

1 cup chicken stock

2 Tbsp. light soy sauce

2 Tbsp. cornstarch

● Heat the oil in a wok and cook the chicken 3 minutes. Using a slotted spoon, remove the chicken from the oil and drain on paper towels. Pour the oil from the wok, leaving 3 tablespoons. Add the mushrooms, peppers, scallions, and snow peas to the wok and stir-fry 3 minutes.

● In a bowl, mash the black beans with the ginger, garlic, and sherry. Add to the wok and stir in the chicken stock and soy sauce. Cook 3 minutes. Blend the cornstarch with 4 tablespoons cold water to a paste and stir into the wok. Bring to a boil, add the chicken and cook 5 minutes, stirring. Serve.

Honeyed Chicken Breasts

This honey and ginger sauce has a wonderful taste and aroma, and complements the poultry perfectly. Try using turkey as a substitute for chicken for equally delicious results.

SERVES 4

1 Tbsp. vegetable oil

2 Tbsp. butter

4 half chicken breasts, boned

1 garlic clove, minced

2 leeks, sliced

1 red bell pepper, cut into strips

½ cup baby corn, halved lengthwise

2 Tbsp. soft brown sugar

4 Tbsp. honey

1 cup chicken stock

2 Tbsp. light soy sauce

3 pieces bottled stem ginger, sliced

2 Tbsp. juice from bottled ginger

2 Tbsp. garlic wine vinegar

2 Tbsp. cornstarch

● Heat the oil and butter in a skillet until the butter has melted. Add the chicken and cook 5 minutes, turning. Add the garlic and leeks and cook a further 3 minutes. Stir in the red pepper, baby corn, sugar, honey, stock, soy sauce, stem ginger, ginger syrup, and vinegar.

● Reduce the heat to a simmer and cook until the chicken is well cooked through, 20 minutes. Blend the cornstarch with 4 tablespoons cold water and stir into the skillet. Bring to a boil and cook until the sauce is thickened and clear. Cook a further 2 minutes and serve.

Spicy Chicken Fry

In this recipe, strips of tender chicken are tossed in soy sauce and coated in bread crumbs, then crisply fried and enjoyed with the tangy dip.

SERVES 4

12 oz chicken breast meat, skinned

3 Tbsp. light soy sauce

3 Tbsp. cornstarch

1 egg, beaten

2 cups fresh white bread crumbs

1 tsp. ground cumin

1 tsp. garam masala

½ tsp. turmeric

½ tsp. chile powder

oil for deep frying

For the Soy Sauce Dip

2 Tbsp. dark soy sauce

⅔ cup chicken stock

2 Tbsp. vermouth

1 tsp. ground ginger

½ tsp. dried lemon grass

1 Tbsp. lemon juice

1 Tbsp. cornstarch

● Cut the chicken into thin strips. Toss in the soy sauce and then roll in the cornstarch.

● Place the beaten egg in a shallow bowl. Mix the bread crumbs, cumin, garam masala, turmeric, and chile powder in another. Coat the chicken first in the egg, then the bread crumb mixture.

● Heat the oil for deep frying to 325°F. Fry the chicken in two batches until golden, 5 minutes. Remove with a slotted draining spoon, drain on paper towels and keep warm whilst the remaining chicken is cooking.

● Meanwhile, place the sauce dip ingredients in a saucepan. Bring to a boil and simmer 3 minutes. Serve with the chicken.

Stir-fried Duck

A very simple dish, making good use of a less frequently used bird. Duck is perfect when cooked with slightly sweet red currant jelly and raisins in this risotto-style recipe.

SERVES 4

10 oz duck breast, skinned

2 Tbsp. vegetable oil

1 red onion, sliced

2 garlic cloves, minced

1 tsp. Chinese five spice powder

1 leek, sliced

⅓ cup raisins

1 red bell pepper, cut into thin strips

2 Tbsp. red currant jelly

2 Tbsp. dark soy sauce

1 cup open cap mushrooms, peeled and sliced

scant 1 cup arborio rice

3¾ cups chicken stock

salt and ground black pepper

2 Tbsp. chopped fresh parsley

● Cut the duck into thin strips. Heat the oil in a large skillet and stir-fry the duck, onion, garlic, Chinese five spice, and leek 5 minutes. Add the raisins, pepper, red currant jelly, soy sauce, mushrooms, and rice and cook 2 minutes, stirring.

● Pour in the stock, season and cook until the liquid has been absorbed and the rice is cooked, 30 minutes. Sprinkle with parsley and serve.

Stir-fried Duck ▶

Lemon Chicken

This recipe has a delicious piquant sauce which sets the taste buds going. It's as pleasing to the palate as it is to the eye with its colorful array of vegetables.

SERVES 4

8 boned chicken thighs

1 Tbsp. vegetable oil

2 Tbsp. butter

1 onion, cut into 16 pieces

1 green bell pepper, cut into strips

1 inch piece fresh ginger root, shredded

⅔ cup chicken stock

juice and grated rind of 1 lemon

1 Tbsp. light soy sauce

1 Tbsp. soft brown sugar

½ cup asparagus spears, trimmed

● Skin the chicken thighs. Heat the oil and butter in a skillet and fry the chicken 10 minutes, turning.

● Add the onion, pepper, and ginger and cook 5 minutes, stirring. Add the stock, lemon juice, soy sauce, and sugar to the skillet. Bring to a boil, reduce the heat and simmer 15 minutes. Add the asparagus and cook 10 minutes. Serve immediately sprinkled with the lemon rind.

Orange Turkey Pan-fry

This orange sauce has an almost caramelized flavor, with the addition of maple syrup and brown sugar which bubble away to perfection with the orange juice and spices.

SERVES 4

1 Tbsp. vegetable oil

4 turkey scallops, skinned

2 garlic cloves, minced

½ tsp. ground cumin

½ tsp. ground coriander

1 leek, sliced

1 green bell pepper, cut into strips

⅔ cup orange juice

2 Tbsp. light soy sauce

⅔ cup chicken stock

2 Tbsp. soft brown sugar

2 Tbsp. maple syrup

1 orange, peeled and sectioned

1 Tbsp. cornstarch

parsley sprigs

● Heat the oil in a skillet and fry the turkey 10 minutes, turning until browned.

● Add the garlic, spices, leek, and pepper and stir-fry 3–4 minutes. Add the orange juice, soy sauce, and chicken stock and bring to a boil. Stir in the brown sugar and syrup, reduce the heat and simmer 20 minutes.

● Add the orange sections to the skillet. Blend the cornstarch with 2 tablespoons cold water to form a smooth paste. Add to the skillet and bring to a boil, stirring until thickened and clear. Cook 1 minute and serve garnished with parsley.

34

Chicken with Mustard Sauce

Wholegrain mustard is used here for a strong flavor with added texture. Any strong mustard could be used in the recipe if preferred.

● Heat the oil in a large skillet and cook the garlic 1 minute. Cut the chicken into 1 inch cubes, add to the pan, and cook 2–3 minutes, stirring.

● Add the fennel, soy sauce, and butter, and stir-fry 5 minutes. Stir in the cream, mushrooms, and mustard, and cook 5 minutes. Sprinkle with chopped chives. Season and serve.

SERVES 4

1 Tbsp. vegetable oil

2 garlic cloves, minced

1 lb chicken breast, boned and skinned

1 fennel bulb, trimmed and sliced

2 Tbsp. light soy sauce

¼ cup butter

⅔ cup heavy cream

2½ cups open cap mushrooms, peeled and sliced

2 Tbsp. wholegrain mustard

3 Tbsp. chopped fresh chives

salt and ground black pepper

Chinese Cashew Casserole

Soy sauce is excellent in casseroles, its piquancy adding a hint of Asia to this cashew nut and chicken dish.

● Heat the oil in a large skillet. Add the chicken and cook until browned, 10 minutes. Remove with a slotted draining spoon and place in an ovenproof casserole dish.

● Heat the oven to 350°F. Add the shallots, mushrooms, turnips, celery, and carrot to the skillet and cook 5 minutes, stirring. Add the flour and cook 1 minute.

● Gradually add the stock, soy sauce, and wine, then bring to a boil, stirring. Add the cashew nuts and tomato paste and season well. Pour onto the chicken in the casserole dish. Cover and cook in the oven, 45 minutes.

● Place the dumpling ingredients in a bowl. Stir in ½ cup cold water and bring together to form a dough. Divide into eight and roll into balls.

● Uncover the casserole and place the dumplings on top of the chicken mixture. Return to the oven, uncovered, until cooked through, 15 minutes. Serve.

SERVES 4

2 Tbsp. sunflower oil

4 chicken pieces

8 shallots

2 cups chestnut mushrooms, quartered

1 cup baby turnips

2 celery stalks, sliced

1 carrot, diced

¼ cup all-purpose flour

2½ cups chicken stock

2 Tbsp. light soy sauce

⅔ cup dry white wine

½ cup unsalted cashew nuts

1 Tbsp. tomato paste

salt and ground black pepper

For the Dumplings

1 cup self-rising flour

½ cup shredded beef suet

1 Tbsp. light soy sauce

1 Tbsp. chopped fresh rosemary

Chinese Cashew Casserole ▶

36

Chicken Curry with Coconut and Lime

All the different flavors in this exotic tasting curry marry wonderfully to produce a slightly sweet sauce with a definite kick provided by the chile. If you think it may be too hot, simply reduce the quantity of chile added.

SERVES 4

1 Tbsp. vegetable oil

2 garlic cloves, minced

1 red onion, halved and sliced

½ tsp. garam masala

½ tsp. ground cumin

½ tsp. ground coriander

½ tsp. dried lemon grass

½ tsp. mild curry powder

¼ tsp. turmeric

1 red chile, chopped

12 oz chicken breast, boned and skinned

1¼ cups chicken stock

1¼ cups coconut milk

2 Tbsp. light soy sauce

juice and grated rind of 1 lime

2 Tbsp. shredded coconut

2 Tbsp. chopped fresh cilantro

● Heat the oil in a large skillet and cook the garlic and onion 5 minutes. Stir in the spices and chile and cook 2 minutes. Slice the chicken breast and add to the skillet. Stir-fry 5 minutes.

● Stir in the stock, coconut milk, soy sauce, and lime juice. Bring to a boil, reduce the heat and simmer until the chicken is cooked through, 20 minutes. Sprinkle with lime rind and cilantro. Serve with rice.

Chicken, Apricot, and Cilantro Casserole

A little Middle Eastern in character, this casserole uses plump dried apricots and herbs to enhance its flavor. Using dried fruits that do not require pre-soaking cuts preparation down to a minimum.

SERVES 4

2 Tbsp. vegetable oil

4 chicken quarters

12 baby onions

1 tsp. ground cinnamon

1 tsp. ground coriander

1-inch piece fresh ginger root, shredded

2½ cups chicken stock

1 Tbsp. light soy sauce

16 dried apricots

6 oz asparagus spears, trimmed

2 Tbsp. cornstarch

salt and ground black pepper

2 Tbsp. chopped fresh cilantro

● Heat the oil in a large skillet and cook the chicken 15 minutes, turning until browned. Remove the chicken with a draining spoon and place in a large ovenproof casserole dish.

● Heat the oven to 350°F. Add the onions, cinnamon, ground coriander, and ginger to the skillet and cook 5 minutes. Transfer to the casserole dish and stir in the stock, soy sauce, and dried apricots. Cover and cook in the oven, 45 minutes.

● Remove the casserole from the oven and stir in the asparagus. Return to the oven until the chicken has cooked through, about 30 minutes. Blend the cornstarch with 2 tablespoons cold water. Remove the casserole from the oven and stir in the cornstarch paste and cilantro. Reheat to thicken, season well, and serve.

39

◄ *Chicken Curry with Coconut and Lime*

Turkey Breast Roll

An easy-to-make dinner party dish. It looks impressive, and has a taste to match. The dish to choose if you want to surprise your guests.

SERVES 8

1 boned turkey breast joint, rolled – approximately
  3 lb in weight

8 slices smoked bacon

2 Tbsp. maple syrup

1 Tbsp. light soy sauce

For the Stuffing

2 cups fresh white bread crumbs

⅔ cup dried peaches, chopped

¼ cup walnut pieces, chopped

1 small carrot, shredded

2 scallions, chopped

1 zucchini, shredded

1 green chile, finely chopped

½ tsp. paprika

2 Tbsp. light soy sauce

2 Tbsp. chopped fresh thyme

● Heat the oven to 375°F. Unroll the turkey joint. Place the bread crumbs for the stuffing in a bowl and add the peaches, walnuts, carrot, scallions, zucchini, chile, paprika, soy sauce, and thyme. Mix together to form a soft stuffing. Use the stuffing to fill the turkey breast, re-roll, and secure with string.

● Lay the bacon slices across the turkey breast. Mix together the maple syrup and soy sauce and spoon over the top. Place the turkey on a trivet in a baking pan and cover. Cook in the oven, 1½ hours. Carve and serve with fresh vegetables.

Brandied Chicken Thighs

Skinned chicken thighs are ideal for pan-fried recipes. Being small in size and pure meat, they cook quickly and are a handy portion size.

SERVES 4

1 Tbsp. vegetable oil

2 onions, quartered

8 chicken thighs, skinned

1 cup shiitake mushrooms

1 red bell pepper, thinly sliced

½ cup green beans

⅔ cup chicken stock

3 Tbsp. brandy

1 Tbsp. light soy sauce

⅔ cup heavy cream

2 tsp. mixed peppercorns, lightly crushed

● Heat the oil in a large skillet and cook the onions and chicken 10 minutes, stirring.

● Add the mushrooms, red pepper, beans, and stock, and cook 2–3 minutes. Remove from the heat and stir in the brandy, soy sauce, cream, and peppercorns. Reduce the heat and cook 20 minutes. Serve.

Duck with Bacon and Red Currants

Smoked bacon adds a lot of flavor of its own to recipes. It is fairly strong and need only be used in small quantities. In this dish it blends perfectly with the duck and red currants.

● Heat the oven to 350°F. Place the bacon in a shallow flameproof casserole and cook over a moderate heat 2–3 minutes. Add the oil and duck breasts and cook 5 minutes, turning until browned.

● Stir in the stock, red currant jelly, soy sauce, and celery. Season and bring to a boil. Cover and cook in the oven until the duck is cooked through, 30 minutes.

● Blend the cornstarch with 8 teaspoons cold water and stir into the dish. Boil until thickened and clear. Season and serve garnished with celery leaves and red currants.

SERVES 4

¾ cup chopped smoked bacon

1 Tbsp. vegetable oil

4 half duck breasts

2 cups chicken stock

4 Tbsp. red currant jelly

1½ Tbsp. light soy sauce

3 celery stalks, sliced

4 tsp. cornstarch

salt and ground black pepper

celery leaves and red currants (optional)

Duck with Bacon and Red Currants ▼

Duck Croustades and Plum Sauce

Duck is ideal served with a tart fruit sauce such as this to balance the flavors.

SERVES 4

4 duck breasts, skinned

1 Tbsp. vegetable oil

2 Tbsp. dark soy sauce

½ tsp. Chinese five spice powder

¼ tsp. ground star anise

For the Sauce

8 oz plums, peeled, pitted, and chopped

⅔ cup vegetable stock

5 Tbsp. port

1 tsp. ground allspice

2 tsp. dark soy sauce

1 Tbsp. cornstarch

For the Croustades

8 slices white bread

¼ cup butter

1 garlic clove, minced

● Shred the duck into thin strips. Heat the oil in a skillet and stir-fry the duck, soy sauce, and spices 10 minutes or until cooked. Remove and keep warm.

● Add the plums, stock, port, allspice, and soy sauce to the skillet. Bring to a boil and simmer until the plums are soft, 15 minutes. Place in a food processor, blend 10 seconds, strain, and return to the pan. Blend the cornstarch with 2 tablespoons cold water and stir into the sauce. Bring to a boil, stirring until thickened and clear. Cook 1 minute and keep warm.

● Meanwhile, cut a 4-inch circle from each slice of bread. Melt the butter in a skillet and cook the garlic and bread rounds 2–3 minutes, turning until golden.

● For each serving, place two bread rounds onto a plate, top with the duck, and serve with plum sauce.

Chicken Filo Pie

Filo pastry is easy and convenient to use for both sweet and savory dishes. Bought prepared and frozen, it may be re-frozen after thawing, so there is no wastage.

SERVES 6

8 sheets of filo pastry, thawed

2 Tbsp. butter, melted

For the Filling

2 Tbsp. butter

1 leek, sliced

1½ cups skinned and chopped chicken breast meat

¼ cup all-purpose flour

¼ cup nibbed almonds, chopped

⅔ cup chicken stock

⅔ cup milk

2 Tbsp. light soy sauce

2 oz sundried tomatoes in oil, drained and sliced

1 celery stalk, sliced

½ cup baby corn, sliced

2 Tbsp. chopped fresh rosemary

ground black pepper

● Melt the butter for the filling in a saucepan and sauté the leek and chicken 5 minutes. Add the flour and cook 1 minute. Stir in the almonds, chicken stock, milk, and soy sauce, and bring to a boil. Add the tomatoes, celery, corn, and rosemary. Season well.

● Heat the oven to 400°F. Place the chicken mixture in a deep pie pan. Lay a sheet of filo pastry on top of the dish and brush with melted butter. Repeat once more. Cut the remaining pastry into triangles and lay on top in layers, brushing with melted butter. Cook in the oven until golden, 20–25 minutes. Serve.

42

Seafood with Soy

Scallops with Pecan Crust

This recipe makes a very rich meal, serve with a light tossed salad, white wine, and fruit.

SERVES 4

2 lb large bay scallops (or sea scallops cut in half)

1¼ cups ground pecans (about 2 cups pecan halves)

1¼ cups fresh bread crumbs

2 eggs

½ cup flour

2 Tbsp. unsalted butter

3 Tbsp. oil

For the Sauce

2 Tbsp. unsalted butter

2 Tbsp. flour

1½ cups white wine

1 Tbsp. light soy sauce

● If the scallops are large, cut them in half. Rinse with cold water and then pat dry using paper towels. The drier they are, the better the coating will stick. Place the ground pecans into a bowl with the bread crumbs and stir. In a separate bowl, lightly beat the eggs. Put the flour in a third bowl. To coat the scallops, first roll each one in the flour, then dip in the egg, and finally roll in the pecan mixture. Make sure each scallop is thoroughly coated.

● Melt the butter and oil in a pan and sauté the scallops until golden, about 10 minutes. Using a slotted spoon, remove them to a bowl and keep warm in the oven at 250°F while you make the sauce. Save the pan drippings for the sauce.

● For the sauce, add the 2 tablespoons butter to the pan drippings and stir until melted. Add the flour, stirring constantly until a smooth paste. Slowly stir in the wine, a little at a time, mixing well. Add the soy sauce. Simmer for about 5 minutes. It should be thick enough to coat a spoon, but not too thick. Spoon the sauce over the scallops and serve.

Crab Cakes

Serrano peppers are small, very hot peppers. Substitute one jalapeño pepper if necessary. The chiles make these crab cakes quite hot; add more or less to suit your own heat tolerance.

MAKES 4 LARGE OR 6 SMALL CRAB CAKES

2 6-oz cans white crab meat

2 fresh serrano chiles, seeded and minced

1½ Tbsp. finely chopped fresh cilantro

1 cup bread crumbs

1 Tbsp. finely chopped onion

1 Tbsp. Dijon-style mustard

1 Tbsp. mayonnaise

1½ tsp. light soy sauce

¼ tsp. pepper

1 tsp. butter

1 tsp. corn oil

● Empty the crab meat with juice into a large bowl. Using a fork, mix in the remaining ingredients, stirring thoroughly. Store in the refrigerator for a few hours or overnight, to allow flavors to blend.

● To cook, form into patties – four large or six small. Sauté lightly in the butter and oil, about 5–7 minutes per side. Serve with tartar sauce or cocktail sauce, if desired.

Cajun-style Shrimp

This dish improves the longer you allow it to marinate. Make it on a weekend and you won't have to cook one night during the week. Just heat up some French bread and serve.

SERVES 4

2 lb fresh shrimp

1 Tbsp. Cajun seasonings

20 pearl onions

2 green bell peppers, sliced into bite-size squares

2 cups sliced fresh mushrooms

⅓ cup bottled chile sauce

⅓ cup red wine vinegar

⅓ cup olive oil

1 tsp. catsup

1 Tbsp. sugar

2 tsp. salt

3 Tbsp. Worcestershire sauce

1 Tbsp. light soy sauce

2 bay leaves

dash of Tabasco sauce

● Peel and clean the shrimp. Steam them over a pan of boiling water into which the Cajun seasonings have been added, about 10 minutes or until done.

● In a separate pan, boil the pearl onions 8 minutes. Drain and rinse with cold water. When they are cool enough to handle, cut off the root end. Squeeze the other end until the peeled center pops out. In a bowl, mix the shrimp, green peppers, peeled onions, and mushrooms, and toss to mix well.

● Thoroughly mix together the chile sauce, vinegar, oil, catsup, sugar, salt, Worcestershire sauce, soy sauce, bay leaves, and Tabasco. Pour over the shrimp and vegetables and stir. Store in the refrigerator for 24 hours or longer, turning occasionally so that all ingredients are thoroughly marinated. Serve cold.

Soy-baked Shrimp

This elegant shrimp dish is perfect for company or special occasions. Prepare the shrimp up to a day ahead of time, minus the sherry, and cover and store in the refrigerator. Add the sherry and bake at mealtime.

SERVES 6

1 quart water

2 tsp. ground thyme

2 tsp. ground cumin

2 lb. unpeeled small shrimp (about 50–60)

¼ cup melted butter

2 tsp. light soy sauce

½ cup finely chopped red onion

1½ cups fresh bread crumbs

1 tsp. dried thyme leaves

¼ cup minced fresh cilantro

6 Tbsp. sherry

● In a large pan, mix the water, thyme, and cumin, and bring to a boil. Add the shrimp and cook until tender, about 5 minutes. Drain, peel, and devein the shrimp and divide them between six individual ovenproof serving bowls or ramekins.

● Heat the oven to 375˚F. Melt the butter in a small saucepan, add the soy sauce, and sauté the red onion 3–4 minutes until softened. Put the bread crumbs in a bowl and stir in the melted butter, soy sauce, and onion until uniformly moistened. Stir in the thyme and cilantro.

● Divide the bread crumb mixture evenly between the six ramekins, topping the shrimp. Pour 1 tablespoon sherry over each. Bake in the oven 20 minutes.

Barbecued Fish Steaks ▲

Barbecued Fish Steaks

Thick fish steaks or fillets, such as cod, salmon, or tuna, are ideal for this recipe because they are firmer and will not break up during cooking.

● Place the fish in a shallow dish. Mix together the oil, vinegar, sugar, soy sauce, wine, garlic, and fennel seeds. Pour over the fish, cover, and marinate 3 hours or overnight.

● Remove the fish from the marinade and place a piece of fish in the center of four squares of aluminum foil or parchment paper. Divide the vegetables and lime rind between the fish and bring the foil or paper round to form a parcel. Spoon 2 tablespoons of the marinade over each and seal completely. Cook on hot barbecue coals or broil until cooked through, 10–15 minutes. Serve hot with salad.

SERVES 4

4 6-oz fish steaks, such as cod, sea bass, salmon, or swordfish, at least 1-inch thickness

⅔ cup salad oil

⅔ cup red wine vinegar

1 Tbsp. soft brown sugar

2 Tbsp. light soy sauce

¼ cup dry white wine

1 garlic clove, minced

1 tsp. fennel seeds

1 head fennel, trimmed and cut into 8 pieces

2 celery stalks, cut into strips

1 red onion, cut into 8 pieces

grated rind of 1 lime

Fish Bites

Use a really "meaty" fish for cubing in this recipe. Wrap the wooden skewers in foil or soak them in cold water before use to prevent them from burning.

SERVES 4

10 oz firm white fish, cubed	For the Sauce
2 Tbsp. light soy sauce	⅔ cup dry white wine
1 Tbsp. lemon juice	5 Tbsp. fish stock
2 Tbsp. dry white wine	1 Tbsp. light soy sauce
½ tsp. ground ginger	2 Tbsp. ginger wine
1 large zucchini	1 tsp. fresh ginger root, shredded
1 large carrot	1 Tbsp. cornstarch
1 Tbsp. chopped fresh dill	2 scallions, chopped

● Place the fish in a shallow dish. Mix together the soy sauce, lemon juice, white wine, and ginger. Pour over the fish, cover, and marinate 2 hours, turning occasionally.

● Meanwhile, using a vegetable peeler, slice the zucchini and carrot lengthwise into thin strips. Blanch in boiling water 1 minute and then plunge them into cold water. Leave until cold. Soak four wooden skewers in cold water 30 minutes.

● Remove the fish from the marinade, reserving the marinade, and the vegetable strips from the water. Pat the vegetables dry with paper towels.

● Wrap a piece of zucchini around each fish cube and then a piece of carrot. Thread four cubes onto each wooden skewer and brush with marinade. Broil 10 minutes, turning once and brushing with the marinade.

● Make the sauce, heat the wine, stock, soy sauce, ginger wine, and ginger in a pan. Bring to a boil. Blend the cornstarch with 2 tablespoons cold water and add to the pan. Return to a boil until thickened and clear, add the scallions, and cook 1 minute. Sprinkle the fish with dill and serve with the sauce.

◀ *Fish Bites*

Fish Curry

A perfect blend of spices and soy sauce make a truly delicious sauce for this dry curry made with red lentils. These lentils are ideal as they do not require pre-soaking and may be used directly after washing.

SERVES 4

12 oz chunky white fish, such as cod

1 Tbsp. vegetable oil

1 onion, halved and sliced

2 garlic cloves, minced

½ tsp. chile powder

½ tsp. ground cumin

½ tsp. ground coriander

1 tsp. garam masala

½ tsp. turmeric

2 Tbsp. light soy sauce

½ cup red lentils

3 cups fish stock

1 red chile, chopped

⅔ cup natural yogurt

chopped fresh cilantro

● Skin the fish and cut the flesh into chunks. Heat the oil in a skillet or wok and lightly sauté the onion and garlic 3–4 minutes, stirring. Add the spices and soy sauce and cook 1 minute.

● Wash the lentils and drain well. Add the stock to the pan and bring to a boil. Reduce the heat and simmer 30 minutes. Add the cubed fish and red chile pan and stir to mix into the curry. Cook until the lentils and fish are cooked, 10 minutes. Stir in the yogurt and sprinkle with cilantro. Serve with whole-wheat rice.

Rice-stuffed Squid

Squid can be bought cleaned and prepared, so eliminating the slightly tricky preparation they require. They are the perfect seafood to complement the olive and rice stuffing, which has a distinctly Greek character to it.

SERVES 4

1 lb baby squid, prepared and cleaned

generous ¼ cup mixed wild and white rice

1¼ cups fish stock

2 Tbsp. light soy sauce

1 small carrot, diced

1 Tbsp. baby corn, sliced

¼ cup chestnut mushrooms, diced

1 Tbsp. black pitted olives, chopped

1½ Tbsp. capers, chopped

1 garlic clove, minced

olive oil for brushing

● Chop the squid tentacles and place in a pan. Add the rice, fish stock, soy sauce, carrot, corn, and mushrooms. Cook until the rice is cooked and the liquid absorbed, about 20 minutes. Add the olives, capers, and garlic to the rice.

● Use the rice mixture to stuff the squid, securing the open end with a toothpick. Brush the squid with oil and broil 5–6 minutes, turning until cooked. Serve.

Sweet and Sour Fish

You can't beat a homemade sweet and sour sauce, especially when it coats chunks of tender, fried fish. The cornstarch helps to keep the fish in one piece and gives it a delicious crispy coating.

SERVES 4

1 lb cod fillet or haddock

1 tsp. rice wine or sherry

1 tsp. light soy sauce

1 egg, beaten

1 cup cornstarch

oil for frying

1 cup canned bamboo shoots, drained and chopped

1 red bell pepper, cut into thin strips

2 garlic cloves, minced

1 tsp. sesame oil

For the Sauce

4 Tbsp. soft brown sugar

2 Tbsp. vegetable oil

6 Tbsp. garlic wine vinegar

2 Tbsp. dark soy sauce

2 tsp. cornstarch

½ tsp. paprika

● Skin the fish and cut the flesh into 1 inch cubes. Mix together the rice wine, soy sauce, and egg. Stir in the fish to coat. Remove the fish and roll in the cornstarch to coat.

● Heat the oil in a wok until almost smoking and add the coated fish. Cook until crisp and cooked through, 5 minutes. Remove from the oil with a slotted spoon and drain on paper towels. Discard the hot oil, leaving approximately 2 tablespoons in the wok. Add the vegetables and garlic and stir-fry 4 minutes. Add the fish and mix well.

● Place the sauce ingredients in a pan and stir well. Heat gently and pour over the fish mixture. Pour on the sesame oil and serve.

Sweet and Sour Fish ▶

Chile Cod and Avocado Salsa

This is a dish with a real Mexican theme, and is fairly hot and spicy. The avocado salsa is a perfect heat extinguisher with its creamy, mild flavor.

SERVES 4

4 cod fillets, skinned

1 Tbsp. lime juice

1 onion, chopped

1 red bell pepper, chopped

2 garlic cloves, minced

2 red chiles, chopped

2 Tbsp. light soy sauce

⅔ cup fish stock

1 tsp. chile powder

For the Guacamole

1 large ripe avocado

2 Tbsp. lemon juice

1 tomato, seeded and chopped

1 onion, finely chopped

ground black pepper

● Make up the avocado salsa. Halve and seed the avocado, peel, and place in a food processor. Add the lemon juice and blend 10 seconds until smooth. Transfer to a bowl and add the tomato and onion. Season well. Cover and chill until required.

● Place the cod fillets on four large squares of aluminum foil. Place the lime juice, onion, red pepper, garlic, chiles, soy sauce, fish stock, and chile powder in a food processor and blend 10 seconds. Spread onto the cod and wrap the foil around the fish to seal completely. Broil 10–15 minutes and serve with the avocado salsa.

◀ Chile Cod and Avocado Salsa

Filo Fish Parcels

These parcels are just bursting with shellfish and seafood in a creamy chive sauce. Fresh is always best, but the frozen mixed seafood available is an economical way to enjoy some of the more exotic seafood without the worry of preparation.

SERVES 4

16 sheets filo pastry

3 Tbsp. butter, melted

For the Filling

2 Tbsp. butter

¼ cup all-purpose flour

⅔ cup fish stock

⅔ cup heavy cream

1 Tbsp. light soy sauce

2 tsp. lemon juice

few drops of Tabasco sauce

1 lb seafood cocktail, thawed if frozen, or 8 oz fresh mussels, clams, shrimp, and squid, prepared

2 Tbsp. chopped fresh chives

salt and ground black pepper

● Melt the butter for the filling in a pan, add the flour, and cook 1 minute. Remove from the heat and stir in the fish stock, cream, soy sauce, lemon juice, Tabasco sauce to taste, and seafood. Bring to a boil and cook 5 minutes. Stir in the chives and season well. Let cool slightly.

● Heat the oven to 425°F. Lay four sheets of filo pastry on a work surface. Brush with melted butter and place another sheet on top of each. Repeat twice more. Spoon one quarter of the fish mixture into the center of each pastry sheet. Brush the edges with butter and bring the edges up to enclose the filling. Scrunch together at the top to form a "purse" shape.

● Brush the parcels with butter and place on a baking sheet. Bake in the oven until golden, 10 minutes. Serve warm.

Coconut Shrimp

Lemon grass is the perfect companion to coconut and chile. Use fresh lemon grass if possible; otherwise use the sliced variety in jars.

● Heat the oil in a wok and lightly fry the onion and garlic, 3–4 minutes. Add the coriander, turmeric, chile powder, and lemon grass, and fry 2 minutes, stirring constantly. Stir in the soy sauce, coconut milk, and tomato paste, and simmer 5 minutes.

● Stir in the shrimp and cook 2–3 minutes. Sprinkle with lime rind and shredded coconut and serve.

SERVES 4

3 Tbsp. vegetable oil

1 red onion, halved and sliced

2 garlic cloves, minced

1 tsp. ground coriander

½ tsp. turmeric

1 tsp. chile powder

1 tsp. dried lemon grass

2 Tbsp. light soy sauce

1 cup coconut milk

1 Tbsp. tomato paste

1 lb peeled shrimp

grated rind of 1 lime

shredded coconut

Mixed Fish Casserole

Delicious saffron scones are perfect to complement a fish dish. If you do not have saffron, use a pinch of turmeric in its place, although the flavor will not be quite as good.

● Skin the fish and cut the flesh into cubes. Melt the butter in a saucepan, add the flour, and cook 1 minute. Remove from the heat and add the wine and milk, stirring well. Return to the heat and stir in the soy sauce, horseradish, fish, mushrooms, and green pepper. Season well and bring to a boil, stirring. Transfer the mixture to a shallow ovenproof dish.

● To make the scones, first place the saffron in the boiling water, infuse 10 minutes. Heat the oven to 350°F. Sift the flour into a bowl, rub in the butter to resemble bread crumbs. Stir in the cheese, saffron threads and soaking liquid, and milk. Mix together to form a soft dough. Roll out on a lightly floured surface and cut into eight equal sized rounds. Arrange on top of the fish. Bake in the oven until golden, 45 minutes.

SERVES 4

8 oz cod fillet

8 oz smoked haddock fillet

8 oz trout fillet

2 Tbsp. butter

¼ cup all-purpose flour

½ cup dry white wine

1¼ cups milk

2 Tbsp. light soy sauce

1 Tbsp. creamed horseradish

½ cup button mushrooms, sliced

1 green bell pepper, diced

salt and ground black pepper

For the Scones

a few strands of saffron

1 Tbsp. boiling water

2 cups self-rising flour

¼ cup butter

½ cup shredded Cheddar cheese

⅔ cup milk

Broiled Salmon with Rosemary

You can't beat the aroma and flavor that fresh rosemary gives, but if it isn't available, try to use freeze-dried rosemary, which retains a better color and flavor than other dried varieties.

S E R V E S   4

4 4-oz salmon steaks or 1-lb salmon tail piece, filleted and skinned

For the Marinade

1 Tbsp. cider vinegar

4 garlic cloves, minced

2 Tbsp. light soy sauce

3 rosemary sprigs

6 Tbsp. olive oil

1 Tbsp. lime juice

salt and ground black pepper

● Lay the salmon in a shallow ovenproof dish. Mix together the marinade ingredients and pour over the fish. Cover and marinate at least 2 hours, turning the fish occasionally.

● Remove the salmon from the marinade with the rosemary. Cook under the broiler, turning once or until cooked through, 10–15 minutes. Serve.

Fish Kebabs

Ideal for a summer party, these kebabs make a delicious appetizer or a good alternative to meat.

S E R V E S   4

1½ lb cod fillets or other thick white fish

4 small baking potatoes, quartered

2 red bell peppers, sliced into large squares

12 large mushrooms

3 Tbsp. olive oil

vegetable cooking spray

For the Marinade

3 Tbsp. light soy sauce

2 garlic cloves, minced

few drops of Tabasco sauce

2 Tbsp. olive oil

1 Tbsp. cider vinegar

2 tsp. molasses

1 red chile, sliced

⅔ cup fish stock

● For the marinade, mix together the soy sauce, garlic, Tabasco sauce, olive oil, cider vinegar, molasses, red chile, and fish stock. Cut the fish into 1½–2 inch cubes. Pour the marinade over the fish and marinate in the refrigerator for several hours or overnight.

● Precook the potatoes to shorten barbecuing time. Use either a microwave (4 minutes on high) or boil them, quartered but with skins, until just tender, 10–15 minutes.

● To make the kebabs, use either metal or wooden skewers that have been soaked in water 30 minutes. Thread the fish cubes, potatoes, peppers, and mushrooms onto the skewers, alternating ingredients. Brush the vegetables with olive oil.

● Spray the broiler with vegetable cooking spray to prevent sticking. Barbecue the kebabs over hot coals, approximately 5 minutes per side.

Fish Kebabs ▶

Rice, Pasta, and Noodles

Hot and Sour Beef Noodles

Rice noodles are thinner than egg noodles and have a wonderful, translucent appearance. They require more cooking or "soaking" than egg noodles but it is worth the effort.

SERVES 4

12 oz rice noodles
1 Tbsp. sesame oil

For the Sauce
1 Tbsp. groundnut oil
½ lb round steak, cut into strips
1 red bell pepper, sliced
2 Tbsp. dark soy sauce
1 Tbsp. chile oil
1 Tbsp. Chinese rice vinegar
4 scallions, sliced
1 tsp. soft brown sugar

62

● Soak the rice noodles in warm water 25 minutes. Drain in a colander and toss in the sesame oil.

● Meanwhile, heat the groundnut oil in a wok, and stir-fry the beef and red pepper 7 minutes. Add the soy sauce, chile oil, Chinese rice vinegar, scallions, and sugar. Simmer 5 minutes.

● Place the noodles in a warmed serving dish and spoon on the beef mixture. Serve immediately.

Mushroom Pasta

Different varieties of mushrooms add extra interest to this wonderful pasta sauce. Any tagliatelle may be used in the recipe; try spinach, tomato, or garlic flavors for a change.

SERVES 4

8 oz dried or fresh tagliatelle
1 tsp. salt

For the Sauce
¼ cup butter
2 garlic cloves, minced
1 red onion, quartered
1 cup shiitake mushrooms
1 cup wild mushrooms
1 cup oyster mushrooms
2 Tbsp. dark soy sauce
⅔ cup vegetable stock
2 Tbsp. chopped fresh parsley
ground black pepper

● Cook the pasta in boiling salted water 8–10 minutes if dried and 5 minutes if fresh, until *al dente*.

● Meanwhile, melt the butter in a saucepan and cook the garlic and onion 5 minutes. Add the mushrooms, soy sauce, and stock and cook 4–5 minutes, stirring.

● Drain the pasta and return to the pan. Stir in the mushroom mixture, tossing the pasta to mix thoroughly. Sprinkle with parsley and season well. Spoon into a warmed serving dish and serve immediately.

Salmon and Haddock Rice

There are three varieties of rice in this simple recipe, all adding to the dish in their own way. The wild rice adds a good color, the wholewheat rice a nutty flavor, and the arborio or risotto rice a great texture.

SERVES 4

2 Tbsp. vegetable oil

1 leek, sliced

1 garlic clove, minced

1 tsp. dried lemon grass

1 tsp. curry powder

¼ tsp. turmeric

generous ⅓ cup wild rice

generous ⅓ cup arborio rice

generous ⅓ cup wholewheat rice

8 oz salmon fillet, skinned and cubed

8 oz smoked haddock fillet, skinned and cubed

2 cups fish stock

⅔ cup vermouth

2 Tbsp. light soy sauce

salt and ground black pepper

2 Tbsp. chopped fresh dill

● Heat the oil in a large skillet and sauté the leek and garlic 3 minutes. Add the lemon grass, curry powder, and turmeric, and cook a further 2 minutes. Add the three rices and cook 1 minute, stirring.

● Add the salmon and smoked haddock and pour in the fish stock, vermouth, and soy sauce. Season and bring to a boil. Reduce the heat to a simmer and cook until the rice is cooked through and the liquid has been absorbed, 30 minutes. Sprinkle with chopped dill and serve.

Pork Chow Mein

This is a classic Chinese noodle recipe that uses dried egg noodles, which are easy and quick to cook.

SERVES 4

6 Chinese dried mushrooms

8 oz dried egg noodles

1 egg, beaten

2 Tbsp. vegetable oil

1 lb pork tenderloin, sliced

1 onion, halved and sliced

½ cup canned water chestnuts, drained and sliced

⅔ cup vegetable stock

2 Tbsp. dark soy sauce

¾ cup Chinese cabbage or bok choy, shredded

2 Tbsp. cornstarch

● Soak the Chinese mushrooms in boiling water 15 minutes. Drain. Boil the egg noodles in water according to package instructions. Drain well and keep warm.

● Heat a 6-inch omelet skillet over a moderate heat. Pour in the egg and tilt to cover the base of the pan. Cook 2 minutes until the top of the omelet is set. Turn over and cook a further 2 minutes. Remove from the pan and slice thinly.

● Heat the oil in a wok and stir-fry the pork 5 minutes. Add the onion, water chestnuts, and Chinese mushrooms, and fry 3 minutes. Stir in the stock, soy sauce, and Chinese cabbage. Cook a further 3 minutes.

● Blend the cornstarch with 4 tablespoons cold water and stir into the wok. Bring to a boil, stirring until thickened. Place the noodles on a warmed plate or bowl. Top with the pork mixture. Sprinkle on the omelet and serve.

◀ *Salmon and Haddock Rice*

Bean and Pasta Soup

Pasta is ideal as a filler in soups, making them really chunky and wholesome. Small pasta shapes cook quickly and are easier to eat in a soup than more traditional shapes.

SERVES 4

⅔ cup mixed dried beans, soaked overnight

7½ cups vegetable stock

2 Tbsp. olive oil

1 leek, sliced

2 garlic cloves, minced

scant 1 cup canned chopped tomatoes

3 Tbsp. light soy sauce

1 cup small pasta shapes

ground black pepper

¼ cup freshly grated Parmesan cheese

1 Tbsp. chopped fresh basil

● Drain the soaked beans and rinse under cold running water. Place in a large saucepan and add the stock. Bring to a boil and boil vigorously for 10 minutes. Reduce the heat to a simmer and cook 1½ hours. Remove half of the beans with a draining spoon, place in a food processor, and process for 20 seconds. Return to the pan.

● In a separate pan, heat the oil and sauté the leek and garlic 5 minutes. Add the canned tomatoes and soy sauce and cook 2–3 minutes. Add the tomato mixture to the pan of beans, with the puréed beans. Stir in the pasta and bring to a boil. Cook until the pasta is cooked, about 10 minutes. Season with pepper and ladle into a warm soup tureen. Sprinkle with Parmesan and basil, and serve.

Curried Noodles

Curried vegetables are tossed into egg noodles for a very quick vegetarian dish. Use any combination of vegetables, varying their color and texture for interest.

SERVES 4

1 lb Chinese egg noodles

4 Tbsp. groundnut oil

1 eggplant, sliced and quartered

1 zucchini, sliced

½ cup baby corn, sliced

2 garlic cloves, minced

1 onion, halved and sliced

½ cup okra, scored around the top

1¼ cups coconut milk

¼ tsp. turmeric

1 tsp. chile powder

2 Tbsp. curry paste

1 tsp. soft brown sugar

2 Tbsp. light soy sauce

2 Tbsp. chopped fresh cilantro

● Boil the noodles in water 4–5 minutes if using dried noodles, or 3–5 minutes if fresh. Drain and immerse in cold water until required.

● Meanwhile, heat the oil in a large skillet and sauté the eggplant, zucchini, corn, garlic, onion, and okra 5 minutes. Stir in the coconut milk, spices, curry paste, sugar, and soy sauce. Simmer 5 minutes.

● Drain the noodles and plunge into boiling water. Drain and place in a warmed serving dish. Pour on the vegetable mixture and serve immediately.

Chile Chicken Noodles ▶

Chile Chicken Noodles

This recipe has a wonderful red-colored sauce coating the noodles for a fiery looking dish which tastes as hot as it looks!

● Cook the noodles in boiling water 5 minutes. Drain and place in a bowl of cold water until required. Slice the chicken breast. Heat the oil for deep frying in a wok until almost smoking. Fry the chicken strips 3–4 minutes. Remove with a draining spoon and drain on paper towels.

● Heat the groundnut oil in a wok and cook the spices, garlic, and soy sauce 30 seconds. Drain the noodles and add to the wok with the chile oil, tomato paste, sugar, scallions, bamboo shoots, and chile. Stir in the chicken and cook 4–5 minutes. Serve.

SERVES 4

8 oz thin dried egg noodles

8 oz chicken breast meat

oil for deep frying

1 Tbsp. groundnut oil

1 tsp. Chinese five spice powder

1 tsp. chile powder

2 garlic cloves, minced

2 Tbsp. light soy sauce

1 tsp. chile oil

2 Tbsp. tomato paste

2 tsp. brown sugar

4 scallions, sliced

½ cup canned bamboo shoots, drained

1 red chile, chopped

Hot Pasta Salad

Pasta salads are usually cold but this colorful recipe really benefits from being eaten warm, as it brings out the flavors in the dressing.

SERVES 4

8 oz whole-wheat pasta shapes

1 tsp. salt

1 Tbsp. vegetable oil

1 red bell pepper, sliced

1 green bell pepper, sliced

1 yellow bell pepper, sliced

½ cup snap peas

1 cup small cauliflower flowerets

1 carrot, cut into strips

½ cup sundried tomatoes in oil, drained and sliced

1 Tbsp. sesame seeds

ground black pepper

For the Dressing

2 Tbsp. light soy sauce

¼ cup dry white wine

1 Tbsp. olive oil

1 Tbsp. sesame oil

2 Tbsp. balsamic vinegar

2 Tbsp. chopped fresh thyme or parsley

2 tsp. wholegrain mustard

● Cook the pasta in boiling salted water until *al dente*, 8–10 minutes.

● Meanwhile, heat the oil in a large skillet and stir-fry the peppers, snap peas, cauliflower, carrot, and tomatoes 7 minutes. Place the dressing ingredients in a pan and simmer 2–3 minutes.

● Drain the pasta and place in a warm serving dish. Top with the vegetable mixture and pour on the dressing. Sprinkle with sesame seeds, season with pepper, and toss well. Serve immediately.

◀ *Hot Pasta Salad*

Pasta and Spinach Soufflé

Pasta is very versatile and can be used in many dishes. In this soufflé, it adds texture and bite to the dish. The three colors of the pasta stand out from the golden color of the soufflé.

SERVES 4

4 oz tricolor pasta shapes

½ tsp. salt

1 lb fresh spinach, stems removed

¼ cup butter

3 Tbsp. all-purpose flour

scant 1 cup milk

3 Tbsp. light soy sauce

ground black pepper

dash of ground nutmeg

3 eggs, separated

1 cup shredded Emmenthal cheese

1 egg white

70

● Grease a 5-cup soufflé dish. Cook the pasta in boiling salted water until *al dente*, 8–10 minutes. Drain and reserve. Blanch the spinach 2 minutes in boiling water. Drain well in a sieve, pressing down to remove all the moisture.

● Heat the oven to 375°F. Melt the butter in a saucepan, stir in the flour, and cook 1 minute. Remove from the heat and stir in the milk and soy sauce. Return to the heat and bring to a boil, stirring until thickened. Season with pepper and nutmeg and cool slightly.

● Beat the egg yolks, one at a time, into the sauce with ¾ cup of the cheese. Stir in the drained pasta and spinach.

● Whisk the egg whites until peaks form and fold into the mixture. Spoon into the soufflé dish and sprinkle with the remaining cheese. Stand the dish on a baking sheet. Cook in the oven until risen and set, 30 minutes. Serve immediately.

Spicy Green Rice

There is something very pleasing to both the eye and the palate about a mixture of green vegetables. Perfectly offset by the wild and wholewheat rice, this really is a feast for the eyes.

SERVES 4

2 Tbsp. olive oil

½ cup okra

1 zucchini, cut into thin strips

2 celery stalks, sliced

½ cup green beans, trimmed

1 green bell pepper, cut into strips

1 green chile, sliced

1 tsp. chile powder

1 tsp. ground coriander

1 tsp. garam masala

½ tsp. ground cinnamon

½ cup nibbed almonds

generous ½ cup wild rice

generous ½ cup wholewheat rice

2 Tbsp. light soy sauce

2½ cups vegetable stock

5 Tbsp. heavy cream

2 Tbsp. chopped fresh parsley

ground black pepper

● Heat the olive oil in a skillet and sauté the vegetables 5 minutes. Add the spices, almonds, and rices, and cook 1 minute. Stir in the soy sauce and stock and bring to a boil. Reduce the heat and simmer until all the liquid has been absorbed and the rice is cooked, 30 minutes.

● Stir in the cream and half of the parsley and season. Transfer to a warmed serving dish and sprinkle with remaining parsley. Serve.

Spicy Green Rice ▶

Scrambled Pasta

A complete meal in a pan, this is a perfect brunch or suppertime dish. It is quick to prepare and easy to cook.

SERVES 4

1 cup dried small pasta shapes

½ tsp. salt

1 Tbsp. vegetable oil

4 large flavored sausages, such as leek, pepper, herb, or mustard

6 slices smoked bacon, trimmed and chopped

2 tomatoes, seeded and chopped

6 eggs, beaten

5 Tbsp. milk

1 Tbsp. light soy sauce

1 Tbsp. butter

½ cup shredded Cheddar cheese

2 Tbsp. heavy cream

ground black pepper

● Cook the pasta in boiling salted water until *al dente*, 10 minutes. Drain well.

● Meanwhile, heat the oil in a large skillet and cook the sausages 10 minutes. Remove from the skillet, slice, and return to the skillet with the chopped bacon and tomatoes. Cook 5 minutes, stirring. Stir in the drained pasta.

● Beat together the eggs, milk, and soy sauce. Add the butter to the skillet and pour in the egg mixture. Cook, stirring, 3–4 minutes. Stir in half of the cheese and cook a further 2 minutes. Stir in the cream and spoon the mixture into a warmed serving dish. Sprinkle with remaining cheese, season, and serve.

◀ *Scrambled Pasta*

Cheese and Rice Cobbler

Traditionally a sweet dessert, this cobbler uses four cheeses to flavor the creamy sauce in which the rice is cooked. Topped with crisp bread, dripping with garlic butter, it is a great dish.

SERVES 4

For the Herb Butter

¼ cup butter, softened

3 Tbsp. chopped fresh mixed herbs, such as parsley, thyme, basil, and sage

4 slices white bread, cut into 16 triangles, crusts removed

For the Rice Mixture

generous 1 cup long grain white rice

2½ cups vegetable stock

2 Tbsp. soy sauce

1 cup open cap mushrooms, sliced

1 Tbsp. chopped fresh parsley

½ cup shredded Parmesan cheese

½ cup shredded Emmenthal cheese

½ cup shredded Gruyere cheese

½ cup shredded Mozzarella cheese

ground black pepper

scant 1 cup heavy cream

● Make up the herb butter by mixing together the softened butter and herbs. Place in a dish and chill until required.

● Place the rice, stock, soy sauce, mushrooms, and parsley in a large skillet and cook 20 minutes.

● Heat the oven to 375°F. Mix together the four cheeses and sprinkle onto the rice. Mix well and spoon into a shallow ovenproof dish. Season the cream and pour onto the rice.

● Arrange the bread triangles on top of the rice around the dish edge. Spoon the herb butter on top. Bake in the oven until the bread is crisp, 30 minutes. Serve.

Noodles with Peanut Sauce

Noodles tossed in a spicy peanut sauce with vegetables make a quick vegetarian satay dish.

SERVES 4

½ lb broccoli flowerets

1 carrot, cut into strips

1 leek, sliced

1 zucchini, sliced

4 scallions, sliced

1 green chile, sliced

2 Tbsp. groundnut oil

⅔ cup crunchy peanut butter

scant 1 cup coconut milk

1 Tbsp. lime juice

2 Tbsp. light soy sauce

1 Tbsp. chile sauce

1 lb egg noodles

74

● Cook all the prepared vegetables in the groundnut oil in a wok or large skillet 3–4 minutes.

● Meanwhile, place the peanut butter, coconut milk, lime juice, soy sauce, and chile sauce in a pan. Stir over a low heat until mixed and hot.

● Cook the noodles in boiling water 2–3 minutes. Drain and add to the vegetables. Pour on the peanut sauce and serve immediately.

Pasta Gratin

Brightly colored peppers always look spectacular and, when combined with sundried tomatoes, garlic, and olive oil, give a truly Mediterranean taste.

SERVES 4

12 oz dried pasta bows

1 tsp. salt

1 Tbsp. olive oil

2 garlic cloves, minced

1 red bell pepper, cut into thin strips

1 green bell pepper, cut into thin strips

3 oz sundried tomatoes in oil, drained and cut into strips

2 Tbsp. light soy sauce

⅔ cup heavy cream

1 Tbsp. lemon juice

2 Tbsp. chopped fresh thyme or parsley

1 egg, beaten

ground black pepper

¾ cup shredded Mozzarella cheese

● Cook the pasta in boiling salted water until *al dente*, 8–10 minutes. Drain well.

● Meanwhile, heat the oil in a skillet and fry the garlic, peppers, and tomatoes 5 minutes. Mix the soy sauce, cream, lemon juice, thyme or parsley, and egg. Season. Place the pasta and pepper mixture in a shallow heatproof dish. Pour on the cream mixture.

● Sprinkle the dish with the Mozzarella cheese. Cook under the broiler until browned, 5 minutes. Serve.

CHAPTER FIVE

Main Meat Meals

Lamb Chops with Tomato Relish

A simple fresh tomato and herb relish, spiced up with horseradish, is perfect with juicy tender lamb chops.

SERVES 4

8 lamb rib chops

2 Tbsp. dark soy sauce

1 Tbsp. olive oil

1 garlic clove, minced

2 Tbsp. garlic wine vinegar

2 rosemary sprigs

For the Tomato Relish

4 tomatoes, seeded and chopped

1 Tbsp. soft brown sugar

4 tsp. red wine vinegar

2 scallions, sliced

1 Tbsp. horseradish sauce

1 Tbsp. dark soy sauce

1 Tbsp. chopped fresh rosemary

● Trim the excess fat from each lamb chop. Scrape the bone with a knife until clean. Place the lamb in a shallow dish. Mix together the soy sauce, olive oil, garlic, garlic wine vinegar, and rosemary. Pour over the lamb. Cover and marinate 2 hours.

● Meanwhile, place the relish ingredients in a pan and simmer 5 minutes. Remove the lamb from the marinade and broil 15 minutes, turning until cooked through. Re-heat the tomato relish until hot and serve with the broiled lamb.

78

Lamb Chops with Tomato Relish ▶

Pan-fry Beef with Peppercorn Sauce

This classic recipe benefits greatly from the addition of soy sauce. Always remember to ignite and extinguish the brandy before returning the pan to the heat.

SERVES 4

4 sirloin steaks

3 Tbsp. mixed peppercorns, crushed

2 Tbsp. butter

1 Tbsp. vegetable oil

2 Tbsp. brandy

1 Tbsp. light soy sauce

⅔ cup heavy cream

● Trim the steaks of any excess fat. Press the crushed peppercorns onto each side of the steaks. Heat the butter and oil in a skillet and cook steaks 3 minutes on each side. Remove from the skillet and keep warm.

● Remove the skillet from the heat and add the brandy. Ignite and let burn out. Stir in the soy sauce and cream. Return the steaks to the pan and return to the heat 3–4 minutes. Serve.

Beef and Walnut Casserole

Beef and pickled walnuts are an ideal combination in this rich dark sauce. The crunchy mustard bread topping finishes it off to perfection.

SERVES 4

3 Tbsp. butter

1½ lb lean beef stewing meat, trimmed and cubed

2 garlic cloves, minced

12 pearl onions

4 Tbsp. all-purpose flour

2½ cups dark beer

4 tsp. red wine vinegar

4 Tbsp. dark soy sauce

1¼ cups beef stock

salt and ground black pepper

12 pickled walnuts, drained and halved

8 slices French bread

4 Tbsp. wholegrain mustard

● Heat the oven to 325°F. Melt the butter in a large flameproof casserole dish and sauté the meat, garlic, and onions 5 minutes. Stir in the flour and cook 1 minute. Gradually pour in the dark beer, add the vinegar, soy sauce, and beef stock. Season well and stir in the pickled walnuts.

● Cover and cook in the oven until the beef is cooked through, about 2 hours. Spread the French bread with mustard. Remove the casserole from the oven and uncover. Arrange the bread slices on top and return to the oven, uncovered, 30 minutes. Serve.

81

◄ *Pan-fry Beef with Peppercorn Sauce*

Pork in Filo Parcels

This is a variation on Cordon bleu, using ham and cheese as a topping for meat, but the flavor is slightly Italian because of the sundried tomatoes and herbs.

SERVES 4

4 pork scallops

2 Tbsp. vegetable oil

8 sheets of filo pastry

2 Tbsp. butter, melted

For the Topping

½ cup minced ham

1 Tbsp. light soy sauce

½ cup shredded Mozzarella cheese

1 Tbsp. chopped fresh thyme

1 oz sundried tomatoes in oil, drained and chopped

ground black pepper

● Place the pork scallops between two sheets of wax paper and beat with a meat mallet until ¼ inch in thickness. Cook in the oil in a skillet 10 minutes, turning. Remove from the skillet and drain well on paper towels.

● Heat the oven to 375°F. Mix together the topping ingredients. Lay four sheets of filo pastry side by side on a work surface. Brush with butter. Place a further sheet on top of each. Place a pork scallop in the center of each sheet of pastry and top each with a quarter of the ham mixture.

● Brush the edges of the pastry with butter and fold around the scallop. Brush with butter and place on a baking sheet. Bake in the oven until the parcels are cooked through, about 20 minutes. Serve.

Lamb Hot Pot

The soy sauce really makes the juices in this favorite hot pot extra special.

SERVES 4

1½ lb boned lamb shoulder

3 Tbsp. vegetable oil

1 lb leek, sliced

2 carrots, sliced

1 cup green beans, trimmed

2 lb potatoes, thinly sliced

2 tsp. chopped fresh thyme

salt and ground black pepper

2 Tbsp. dark soy sauce

2 cups lamb stock

⅔ cup dry white wine

● Heat the oven to 325°F. Trim the lamb of any excess fat and cut the meat into 1-inch cubes. Heat the oil in a large skillet and sauté the lamb, turning until browned.

● In a large ovenproof casserole, layer the lamb, leeks, carrots, beans, and potatoes, sprinkling each layer with thyme and seasoning, reserving enough potato to cover the surface. Mix together the soy sauce, stock, and wine. Pour over the meat and top with a layer of potatoes.

● Cover and cook in the oven, 2 hours. Uncover the casserole and increase the temperature to 425°F. Cook the casserole until the potatoes are golden and crisp, 30 minutes. Serve.

Spicy Roast Pork

Tender pork coated in plum glaze and baked with fresh plums looks sensational. As an alternative to pork tenderloin use turkey breast.

● Heat the oven to 350°F. Trim any excess fat from the meat. Heat the oil in a roasting pan over a moderate heat. Add the pork and turn to brown all over. Place the soy sauce, spices, plum preserves, and honey in a saucepan and heat until liquid. Brush over the pork, reserving any remaining glaze.

● Cook the pork in the oven, 30 minutes. Brush with remaining glaze. Return to the oven until cooked through, 25–30 minutes. Arrange the plum quarters around the pork 10 minutes before the end of cooking time. Slice and serve with the cooking liquor.

SERVES 4

1½ lb pork tenderloin

2 Tbsp. vegetable oil

2 Tbsp. dark soy sauce

2 tsp. Chinese five spice powder

1 tsp. ground cumin

½ tsp. chile powder

½ cup plum preserves, sieved

1 Tbsp. honey

4 oz plums, seeded and quartered

Spicy Roast Pork ▼

Lamb with Cranberry Sauce

Cranberries are traditionally associated with turkey, but are just as good with lamb. Use fresh fruit if possible, or frozen cranberries straight from the freezer. If thawed before use, they will disintegrate during cooking.

S E R V E S   4

8 3-oz boned lamb loin chops

2 Tbsp. vegetable oil

1 cup button mushrooms, halved

1¼ cups lamb stock

2 Tbsp. dark soy sauce

4 Tbsp. cranberry sauce

⅔ cup cranberry juice

1 tsp. tomato paste

¼ cup fresh or frozen cranberries

1 Tbsp. chopped fresh cilantro

1½ Tbsp. cornstarch

● Trim the lamb of excess fat. Heat the oil in a large skillet and fry the lamb 5 minutes, turning until browned. Add the mushrooms and cook a further 2–3 minutes. Add the stock, soy sauce, cranberry sauce, cranberry juice, and tomato paste. Simmer 15 minutes, turning the lamb.

● Stir in the cranberries and cilantro. Blend the cornstarch with 2 tablespoons cold water and stir into the skillet. Bring to a boil, stirring until thickened and clear. Serve.

Cassoulet

This is a time-consuming recipe to prepare but once tasted all the effort is immediately appreciated. Be sure to boil the beans vigorously for 10 minutes before use to remove all the toxins.

S E R V E S   4

8-oz piece of smoked bacon

1 lb fresh pork sides

1 Tbsp. vegetable oil

1 onion, sliced

2 garlic cloves, minced

8 oz garlic sausage, cubed

2 Tbsp. tomato paste

2 Tbsp. dark soy sauce

1¼ cups vegetable stock

1⅔ cups dried mixed beans, soaked overnight

salt and ground black pepper

1 bouquet garni

2 cups fresh white bread crumbs

85

● Remove the rind from the bacon. Cube the pork sides. Heat the oil in a large skillet and sauté the onion and garlic 5 minutes. Add the pork and bacon to the skillet with the sausage, cook until browned. Stir in the tomato paste, soy sauce, and vegetable stock. Bring to a boil, stirring.

● Heat the oven to 300°F. Drain the beans from the soaking water, rinse, and drain. Place in a large flameproof casserole. Stir in the contents of the skillet. Pour 1¼ cups cold water into the casserole and bring to a boil. Season and add the bouquet garni.

● Sprinkle one third of the bread crumbs on top of the bean mixture. Cook in the oven, 2½ hours. During cooking, press down the layer of bread crumbs and top with a further layer. Repeat twice. Serve.

◄ *Lamb with Cranberry Sauce*

Beef Pot Roast

Marinating the beef before cooking tenderizes it and allows it to absorb all the flavors fully.

SERVES 4

2-lb joint top round or chuck steak

⅔ cup red wine

1 red onion, cut into 16 pieces

4 garlic cloves, minced

1 Tbsp. peppercorns

1 bay leaf

2 Tbsp. dark soy sauce

2 Tbsp. chopped fresh parsley

2 Tbsp. vegetable oil

⅔ cup beef stock

1 Tbsp. chopped fresh parsley

● Place the beef in a dish. Add the wine, onion, garlic, peppercorns, bay leaf, soy sauce, and chopped parsley. Cover and let marinate 4 hours. Remove the beef from the marinade, reserve the marinade, discarding the bay leaf and peppercorns.

● Heat the oven to 350°F. Heat the oil in a large flameproof casserole. Add the beef and fry 5 minutes, turning until sealed. Stir in the onion and cook 5 minutes. Pour in the reserved marinade and beef stock. Bring to a boil, stirring, 2 minutes.

● Cover the casserole and cook in the oven until the beef is cooked through, 2–2½ hours.

● Remove the beef from the casserole and slice thinly. Place on a serving plate and serve with the cooking liquid from the casserole.

Beef Stir-fry

Dried mushrooms are a little bit of a luxury, but well worth purchasing. They add a unique, strong flavor to dishes and need only be used in small quantities.

SERVES 4

1 lb lean steak

2 Tbsp. vegetable oil

3 Tbsp. dark soy sauce

1 red chile, chopped

½ inch piece fresh ginger root, shredded

2 Tbsp. red wine vinegar

2 Tbsp. cornstarch

For the Stir-fry

4 dried Chinese mushrooms

1 Tbsp. vegetable oil

4 scallions, cut lengthwise

2 celery stalks, sliced

1 carrot, cut into thin strips

1 zucchini, cut into thin strips

1 cup baby corn, halved lengthwise

1 cup cauliflower flowerets

1 Tbsp. chile sauce

● Cut the beef into thin strips, cutting across the grain. Place in a shallow dish. Mix together half of the oil, the soy sauce, chile, ginger, and vinegar and pour over the beef. Cover and marinate 1 hour.

● Remove the beef from the marinade with a draining spoon, reserving the marinade. Roll the beef in the cornstarch.

● Reconstitute the Chinese mushrooms in boiling water, 20 minutes. Drain well. Heat the remaining oil in a wok and stir-fry the beef 4 minutes. Add the scallions, celery, carrot, zucchini, corn, and cauliflower, and stir-fry a further 4 minutes. Add the reserved marinade to the wok with the chile sauce and stir-fry 1 minute. Serve.

Beef Stir-fry ▶

Beef with Pecan Sauce

This is quite an oily sauce which will separate if overcooked. Serve immediately the dish is cooked for perfect results.

● Place the strips of beef in a shallow dish. Add the onion, vinegar, and soy sauce. Cover and marinate 2 hours.

● Heat the oil and butter in a flameproof casserole dish. Remove the beef from the marinade, reserving the onion. Cook the beef in the butter, turning until browned all over, 10 minutes.

● Add the reserved onion, stock, wine, soy sauce, lemon juice, seasoning, and cinnamon. Cover and simmer until the beef is tender, about 1½ hours.

● Mix together the pecans and flour. Stir into the stock with the cream. Simmer 5 minutes, adjust the seasoning, garnish, and serve.

S E R V E S   4

1 lb steak, cut into strips across the grain

1 onion, sliced

3 Tbsp. balsamic vinegar

1 Tbsp. dark soy sauce

For the Sauce

6 Tbsp. olive oil

3 Tbsp. butter

1¼ cups beef stock

⅔ cup red wine

1 Tbsp. soy sauce

4 Tbsp. lemon juice

ground black pepper

1 tsp. ground cinnamon

1½ cups pecan pieces, crushed

1 Tbsp. all-purpose flour

6 Tbsp. heavy cream

2 Tbsp. chopped fresh cilantro

88

Beef Pizza Pie ▲

Kidneys in Sherry Sauce

Kidneys can be a little difficult to prepare, so ask your butcher to core them for you if you are unsure. Be sure to simmer gently; kidneys become tough if overcooked.

● Halve the shallots. Melt the butter and oil in a large skillet and cook the shallots and mushrooms 3–4 minutes. Add the kidneys and celery and cook 5 minutes. Stir in the flour and cook 1 minute. Add the sherry, soy sauce, stock, and Tabasco sauce to taste. Add the bay leaf.

● Cover and simmer until the kidneys are cooked through, 25 minutes. Serve with freshly cooked rice.

SERVES 4

16 shallots

3 Tbsp. butter

1 Tbsp. vegetable oil

2 cups chestnut mushrooms, halved

12 lamb kidneys, skinned and cored

2 celery stalks, sliced

2 Tbsp. all-purpose flour

3 Tbsp. dry sherry

2 Tbsp. dark soy sauce

2 cups lamb stock

a few drops of Tabasco sauce

1 bay leaf

salt and ground black pepper

Beef Pizza Pie

Filled with spicy beef and peppers, this is a really great way to enjoy pizza!

● Heat the oil and fry the onions 3–4 minutes. Add the garlic and beef and fry 5 minutes, stirring. Add the peppers and chile powder and cook 3–4 minutes.

● Add the flour, mix well, and cook 1 minute. Stir in the tomato paste, stock, soy sauce, tomatoes, and oregano. Bring to a boil, reduce the heat, and simmer 30 minutes. Let cool slightly.

● Heat the oven to 425°F. Make up the pizza dough according to package instructions; knead until smooth. Roll out two thirds of the dough on a lightly floured surface and line a greased, 2-inch-deep loose-bottomed pan. Let the dough overhang the pan edge slightly.

● Spoon the beef filling into the dough-lined pan. Roll out remaining dough in a circle large enough to cover the top. Brush edges with water and place on top, sealing with the overhanging dough by rolling the edge over. Brush with egg. Cook in the oven until golden, 30 minutes. Let cool. Remove and serve.

SERVES 8

2 Tbsp. olive oil

2 onions, chopped

1 garlic clove, minced

1½ cups ground beef

1 small red bell pepper, chopped

1 small green bell pepper, chopped

1 tsp. chile powder

¼ cup all-purpose flour

2 Tbsp. tomato paste

⅔ cup beef stock

2 Tbsp. dark soy sauce

14-oz can chopped tomatoes

1 Tbsp. chopped fresh oregano

10-oz package pizza dough mix

1 egg, beaten

Fruity Burgers

These burgers are succulent and slightly sweet, and have a terrific flavor. Use different dried fruits, such as mango or peach, to vary the flavor.

● Place all the ingredients except the oil in a mixing bowl. Bring together with your hands, mixing well, and divide into four equal portions. On a lightly floured board, shape the meat into four flat rounds.

● Heat the oil in a skillet and cook the burgers, turning once until cooked through, 10 minutes. Place each in a burger bun with lettuce, onion, and dill pickles and serve.

SERVES 4

2 cups ground beef

½ onion, shredded

2 Tbsp. dark soy sauce

salt and ground black pepper

½ cup dried apricots, finely chopped

1 Tbsp. chopped fresh cilantro

1 garlic clove, minced

½ tsp. ground coriander

2 Tbsp. vegetable oil

burger buns, salad, onion slices, and dill pickles

Lamb Couscous

Couscous is a creamy, nutty alternative to rice. Used extensively in African recipes, it is easy to cook and steams over the meat sauce for added flavor.

● Drain the garbanzo beans and place in a large pan. Cover with water and bring to a boil. Boil rapidly 10 minutes. Drain and rinse.

● Melt 6 tablespoons of the butter in a large pan. Add the lamb, salt, pepper, ginger, turmeric, cinnamon, cayenne, onions, cilantro, carrot, and turnips. Cook 10 minutes, stirring.

● Add the stock and soy sauce, and stir in the beans. Bring to a boil, cover and simmer 1½ hours.

● Soak the couscous in 2½ cups vegetable stock until the water has been absorbed, about 30 minutes. Line a colander with a clean damp dish towel and place the couscous in a mound in the colander. Steam over the lamb for the last 30 minutes of cooking. Stir in 2 tablespoons melted butter and place on a serving plate. Spoon on the lamb and serve.

SERVES 4

½ cup dried garbanzo beans, soaked overnight, or
    1-lb can cooked garbanzo beans, drained

½ cup butter

1 lb lamb neck, trimmed of fat and cubed

1 tsp. salt

1 tsp. ground black pepper

1 tsp. ground ginger

¼ tsp. turmeric

¼ tsp. ground cinnamon

¼ tsp. cayenne pepper

2 red onions, quartered

2 cilantro sprigs

1 carrot, cut into chunks

4 baby turnips, quartered

2½ cups lamb stock

2 Tbsp. dark soy sauce

8 oz couscous

2½ cups vegetable stock

Lamb Couscous ▶

Soy Salads

Chinese Cilantro Salad

This is a variation on a classic salad, made extra special by the cheese dressing which is poured over the salad ingredients superbly.

SERVES 4

8 oz head Chinese leaves or bok choy

1 ripe avocado, seeded

1 yellow bell pepper, diced

½ bunch cilantro, chopped, about ½ oz

6 scallions, chopped

2 tomatoes, seeded and diced

4 slices bacon, broiled and chopped

1 tsp. sesame seeds

For the Dressing

¼ cup shredded Parmesan cheese

1 Tbsp. sesame oil

4 Tbsp. salad oil

1 garlic clove, minced

1 Tbsp. honey

2 Tbsp. garlic wine vinegar

¼ tsp. Chinese five spice powder

2 tsp. light soy sauce

● Wash the Chinese leaves well and cut into bite-size pieces. Chop the avocado and add to the leaves with the pepper, cilantro, scallions, tomatoes, bacon, and sesame seeds.

● Mix together the dressing ingredients and pour over the salad. Toss and serve.

Chinese Cilantro Salad ▶

Winter Fruit Salad

Exotic fresh fruits make this salad unusual and refreshing. The soy dressing complements the fruit perfectly.

● Mix together the soy sauce, vinegar, lime juice, and sugar. Arrange the lettuce in a serving bowl.

● Add the pineapple, mango, apple, dates, and walnut pieces. Pour the dressing over the top, toss and serve.

SERVES 4

1 Tbsp. light soy sauce

1 Tbsp. cider vinegar

juice of ½ lime

2 tsp. soft brown sugar

8 oz shredded lettuce

10 oz fresh pineapple, peeled, cored, and cut into bite-size pieces

1 mango, peeled, pitted, and cut into chunks

1 green dessert apple, cored and cut into bite-size pieces

¾ cup pitted dates, chopped

2 Tbsp. walnut pieces

Winter Fruit Salad ▼

Sweet Potato Salad

The secret to success with this recipe is perfectly cooked sweet potatoes. If the potatoes are too mushy, the texture of the salad is not as good. When cooked perfectly, a fork inserted into the potato should meet some resistance.

● Boil the sweet potatoes in a pan of water until just tender, about 20 minutes. Cool, peel, and cut into 1-inch cubes. Put the potatoes in a bowl with the celery, green pepper, pineapple chunks, and grapes.

● In a separate bowl, mix the mayonnaise, curry powder, ginger, soy sauce, and vinegar. Gently fold dressing into the potato mixture. Chill before serving.

S E R V E S   6

2 lb sweet potatoes
½ cup thinly sliced celery
½ cup diced green bell pepper
⅔ cup pineapple chunks
½ cup seedless red grapes
¼ cup mayonnaise
1 tsp. mild curry powder
½ tsp. ground ginger
1 tsp. light soy sauce
2 tsp. cider vinegar

Potato Salad

Walnut oil can be purchased in large supermarkets or in gourmet food stores. Olive oil is an acceptable substitute.

● Wash the potatoes and put them in a pot. Fill with water and add the salt. Bring to a boil and cook until tender, but not mushy, 30 minutes. At the same time, hard boil the eggs in a separate pan.

● When the potatoes are done, rinse with cold water and allow to cool until they are able to be touched. While still warm, peel and slice them into one-and-a-half-inch chunks. Peel and chop the eggs and add them to the potatoes.

● To make the dressing, mix the oil, vinegar, soy sauce, mustard, thyme, and marjoram and whisk to blend. Pour the dressing over the warm potatoes and eggs and toss very gently. Marinate in the refrigerator until cool, at least two hours.

● Just before serving, add the diced celery and chopped scallions. Gently stir in the mayonnaise. Add salt and pepper to taste.

S E R V E S   6

2 lb red potatoes
1 tsp. salt
2 hard-boiled eggs, chopped
¾ cup celery
1 cup chopped celery
2 scallions, chopped
⅓ cup mayonnaise
salt and pepper

For the Dressing
¼ cup walnut oil
2 Tbsp. cider vinegar
1 tsp. light soy sauce
1 tsp. Dijon mustard
¼ tsp. dried thyme
⅛ tsp. chopped fresh marjoram

97

Cucumber Salad

Sesame oil has a distinctive taste, so don't substitute any other oil. You can find it in the Asian food section of your supermarket or in gourmet food stores.

SERVES 4

2 cucumbers (about 1½ lb), peeled and sliced

2 Tbsp. salt

1 Tbsp. sesame oil

1½ tsp. vegetable oil

4 tsp. cider vinegar

1½ tsp. light soy sauce

½ tsp. sugar

½ tsp. mild curry powder

1 small garlic clove, minced

● Peel the cucumbers and slice very thinly. Sprinkle with the salt and let sit for 3 hours or longer. Rinse the cucumbers very well and squeeze them with your hands to remove liquid. Rinse and squeeze again. (The cucumber will look wilted.) Place them in a bowl with a lid.

● Mix the sesame and vegetable oils, vinegar, soy sauce, sugar, curry powder, and minced garlic. Whisk to blend. Pour over the cucumber, cover, and store in the refrigerator for several hours or overnight before serving.

Shredded Salad

Celeriac has a strong, fresh aroma and taste and is delicious in this colorful, simple salad. Serve immediately; celeriac discolors with standing.

SERVES 4

1 celeriac

2 zucchini

2 carrots

⅔ cup shredded coconut

ground black pepper

grated rind of 1 lime

For the Dressing

juice of 1 lime

1 Tbsp. light soy sauce

1 garlic clove, minced

1 Tbsp. honey

● Trim the celeriac, peel, and shred finely. Trim and shred the zucchini and carrots, keeping the vegetables separate.

● Arrange the individual vegetables and coconut in small mounds on a large serving platter. Season with pepper.

● Mix together the dressing ingredients and pour over the vegetables. Garnish the salad with lime rind and serve immediately.

Shredded Salad ▶

98

Chinese Vegetable and Omelet Salad

Resembling a raw stir-fry, this colorful salad makes use of Chinese vegetables. Top with shredded omelet for a special finishing touch.

SERVES 4

1 lb young cabbage

oil for deep frying

1 tsp. salt

½ tsp. ground cinnamon

2 cups bean sprouts

4 scallions, halved lengthwise

½ cup canned water chestnuts, drained and chopped

1 red bell pepper, sliced

1 yellow bell pepper, sliced

½ cup salted cashew nuts

For the Omelet

2 eggs

½ tsp. Chinese five spice powder

For the Dressing

2 Tbsp. light soy sauce

1 Tbsp. lime juice

1 Tbsp. sesame oil

½ tsp. ground ginger

● Shred the young cabbage. Heat the oil in a wok and deep fry the greens, 4–5 minutes. Drain well on paper towels and sprinkle with salt and cinnamon. Place in a large serving bowl. Top with the bean sprouts, scallions, water chestnuts, peppers, and cashew nuts.

● Beat the eggs for the omelet with the Chinese five spice. Heat a 6-inch omelet skillet and pour in the eggs, tilting the pan to coat the base with egg. Cook 2 minutes until the top is set. Flip over and cook 2 minutes. Remove and cut into strips. Sprinkle over the vegetables. Mix the dressing, pour on, and serve.

◄ *Chinese Vegetable and Omelet Salad*

Endive, Bacon, and Asparagus Salad

Broiled lettuce, such as Belgian endive, makes a delightful salad, especially when topped with tender asparagus and hot melting cheese.

SERVES 4

2 heads Belgian endive

4 slices smoked bacon

12 oz asparagus spears

¼ cup shredded Emmenthal cheese

1 Tbsp. pine kernels

For the Dressing

1 Tbsp. light soy sauce

1 Tbsp. lemon juice

2 Tbsp. olive oil

1 tsp. prepared mustard

1 Tbsp. garlic wine vinegar

ground black pepper

2 tsp. chopped fresh thyme

● Separate the endive leaves and place in a shallow ovenproof dish. Broil the bacon 10 minutes, turning until crisp; chop roughly. Meanwhile, cook the asparagus in boiling water until tender, 2–3 minutes. Drain well and place on top of the endive leaves. Sprinkle with the bacon, cheese, and pine nuts.

● Mix together the dressing ingredients and pour over the salad. Cook under the broiler until the cheese begins to melt, 3–4 minutes. Serve.

Lamb and Orange Salad

Hot salads are sensational: the mixture of warm and cold ingredients is a treat. In this recipe, tender chunks of lamb are sautéed to perfection in soy sauce and served with fennel and fresh orange.

SERVES 4

1 lb lamb leg steak

1 Tbsp. vegetable oil

1 Tbsp. dark soy sauce

1 fennel bulb, sliced

2 oranges, peeled and sectioned

½ cup pecan halves

4 oz mixed salad leaves, shredded

½ cup cucumber, sliced and quartered

grated rind of 1 orange

For the Dressing

3 Tbsp. olive oil

3 Tbsp. fresh orange juice

½ tsp. prepared horseradish

salt and ground black pepper

2 tsp. honey

1 tsp. fresh rosemary

● Dice the lamb, removing any excess fat. Heat the oil and soy sauce in a skillet. Cook the lamb until cooked through, 10 minutes. Reserve the lamb and cooking liquor.

● Prepare the remaining ingredients and place in a serving bowl. Remove the lamb from the skillet with a draining spoon and add to the salad.

● Mix together the dressing ingredients. Add the cooking liquor from the skillet, stir well, and pour over the salad. Serve.

102

Lamb and Orange Salad ▶

Carrot, Raisin, and Leek Salad

Caraway seeds are used in this semi-sweet salad, being ideal in both sweet and savory dishes. They have a strong, slightly aniseed flavor.

SERVES 4

6 large carrots

3 large oranges

⅓ cup raisins

2 leeks

For the Dressing

⅔ cup fresh orange juice

2 Tbsp. dark soy sauce

1 Tbsp. maple syrup

¼ tsp. ground nutmeg

ground black pepper

1 tsp. caraway seeds

● Trim and shred the carrots and place in a bowl. Peel and section the oranges and add to the carrots. Add the raisins. Trim and thinly slice the leeks and stir into the carrots.

● Mix together the dressing ingredients and pour over the salad. Cover and chill until required.

◄ *Carrot, Raisin and Leek Salad*

Lentil Salad

Lentils make a nutritious and colorful base for a salad. Here they are mixed with spicy vegetables and served cold. This dish would be equally tasty served hot.

SERVES 4

1½ cups red lentils

dash of salt

1 tsp. curry powder

2 cups vegetable stock

2 Tbsp. vegetable oil

1 cup green beans

1 cup diced carrots

½ cup tomatoes, seeded and diced

1 small eggplant, diced

3 garlic cloves, minced

½ tsp. chile powder

¼ tsp. turmeric

½ tsp. ground cumin

½ tsp. ground coriander

2 Tbsp. light soy sauce

2 Tbsp. chopped fresh cilantro

105

● Wash the lentils and place in a large pan with the salt and curry powder. Add the stock and soak 15 minutes. Bring to a boil, reduce the heat, cover, and simmer 15 minutes. Turn off the heat and let stand 5 minutes.

● Meanwhile, heat the oil in a skillet, add the vegetables, garlic, spices, and soy sauce and cook 10 minutes. Switch off the heat and let cool.

● Mix together the lentils and spicy vegetables and sprinkle with chopped cilantro. Serve.

Chicken Salad

Soy sauce and ginger make a really special dressing for this colorful chicken salad.

SERVES 4

10 oz cooked chicken, diced

1 cup canned water chestnuts, drained and sliced

1 cup alfalfa sprouts

2 tomatoes, seeded and diced

4 scallions, sliced

1 green bell pepper, diced

¼ cup unsalted cashew nuts

1 mango, peeled and diced

2 heads of Belgian endive

For the Dressing

1 Tbsp. light soy sauce

1 tsp. ground ginger

2 Tbsp. walnut oil

2 Tbsp. garlic wine vinegar

1 Tbsp. honey

1 Tbsp. chopped fresh parsley

1 tsp. lemon juice

● Place the chicken in a bowl with the water chestnuts, alfalfa sprouts, tomatoes, scallions, pepper, cashew nuts, and mango. Mix together gently.

● Arrange the endive around a serving plate and spoon the chicken mixture into the center.

● Place all the dressing ingredients in a screwtop jar and shake vigorously to mix. Pour over the salad and serve immediately.

Spinach Noodle Salad

Young spinach leaves should be used for this recipe. The small leaves taste and look terrific with the spicy sauce and noodles.

SERVES 4

8 oz flat rice noodles

2 Tbsp. groundnut oil

8 scallions, sliced

2 garlic cloves, minced

½ tsp. star anise, ground

2 tsp. chopped fresh ginger root

2 Tbsp. dark soy sauce

3 oz young spinach leaves, washed

1 Tbsp. sesame oil

2 Tbsp. chopped fresh cilantro

● Cook the noodles in boiling water, 4–5 minutes. Drain and cool in cold water.

● Heat the groundnut oil in a wok and cook half of the scallions, the garlic, star anise, ginger, and soy sauce 2 minutes. Cool completely.

● Arrange the spinach in a serving bowl. Drain the noodles and toss into the vegetables. Sprinkle over the sesame oil and place on top of the spinach. Sprinkle with remaining scallions and serve garnished with fresh cilantro.

Spinach Noodle Salad ▶

CHAPTER SEVEN

Vegetables and Side Dishes

Snow Pea and Mushroom Stir-fry

This is a colorful, nutritious vegetable dish that is quick to cook and ideal with broiled meats and fish.

● Trim the snow peas. Heat the oil in a large skillet or wok and cook the snow peas, corn, broccoli, and leek 5 minutes.

● Stir in the mushrooms, soy sauce, garlic, and sesame seeds, and cook 3 minutes. Add the sesame oil, stirring, and serve.

SERVES 4

1 cup snow peas

1 Tbsp. olive oil

1 cup baby corn, halved lengthwise

1 cup broccoli flowerets

1 leek, sliced

1 cup mushrooms, sliced

2 tsp. light soy sauce

1 garlic clove, minced

2 tsp. sesame seeds

1 tsp. sesame oil

Snow Pea and Mushroom Stir-fry ▶

Green Peppers and Deep-fried Bean Curd

Quick to prepare, this recipe is best served immediately. If you can't find Chinese mushrooms use any large mushrooms.

● Make the sauce. Mix the potato flour, mushroom water, oyster sauce, and soy sauce. Heat a wok, add 2 tablespoons oil and swirl around. Add the garlic, white scallions and Chinese mushrooms. Stir for 30 seconds and pour in potato flour mixture. Reduce heat and continue to stir until the sauce thickens. Remove from heat.

● Heat 1 tablespoon oil in a wok over high heat until smoking. Add the ginger, cabbage, and green pepper. Toss 30 seconds. Season, reduce heat and cook, covered, 2 minutes. Remove and put into a large pan.

● Half fill the wok with oil, heat to 200°F and lower the bean curd into the oil, one at a time, and fry for 4 minutes, turning over occasionally. Remove with a slotted spoon and drain on paper towels.

● Lay the bean curd on the cabbage in the pan and add the green scallions. Heat the sauce and pour over the bean curd. Heat for 2 minutes and serve.

SERVES 4

1 Tbsp. groundnut oil or corn oil

2 thin slices fresh ginger root, peeled

4 large leaves Chinese celery cabbage, shredded

1 large green bell pepper, seeded and diced

oil for deep frying

4 1-inch square cakes bean curd, dried and cut into rectangles

salt

For the Sauce

1 tsp. potato flour

5 Tbsp. mushroom water

2 Tbsp. oyster sauce

2 tsp. light soy sauce

2 Tbsp. vegetable oil

1 garlic clove, finely chopped

2 scallions, cut into small sections, white and green parts separated

4 large dried Chinese mushrooms, soaked, squeezed and cut into thin strips (water to be reserved)

Sweet Potato Muffins

These sweet, moist muffins are good plain or served with honey.

MAKES ABOUT 12

1 lb sweet potatoes, cooked, peeled, and mashed

½ cup butter

½ cup brown sugar

2 eggs

1 Tbsp. baking powder

1 Tbsp. light soy sauce

¼ cup milk

1½ cups flour

● Boil the sweet potato in a pan of water until soft, about 20 minutes. Peel and mash.

● Heat the oven to 375°F. Cream the butter and brown sugar together. Add the mashed sweet potato, eggs, baking powder, and soy sauce. Finally, stir in the milk and flour, and mix thoroughly.

◄ *Sweet Potato Muffins*

Stir-fry Zucchini with Sesame Seeds

With just a little extra effort, you can turn an ordinary vegetable into a treat. Soy sauce brings out the flavor of zucchini and sesame seeds add a slight crunch.

SERVES 4

4 large zucchini (about 2 cups sliced)

2 tsp. olive oil

4 tsp. light soy sauce

½ tsp. dill weed

2 tsp. sesame seeds

● Wash the zucchini and then slice into ⅛ to ¼ inch rounds. Heat the oil in a nonstick pan over medium heat and add the zucchini. Sprinkle the soy sauce and dill weed over the top and sauté 3–4 minutes until the zucchini begins to wilt. Add the sesame seeds and continue cooking until the zucchini starts to brown, about 3 or 4 more minutes. Serve immediately.

113

Vegetable Spring Rolls

These spring rolls are ideal as part of a Chinese meal. Soy sauce gives the vegetables an extra special flavor.

MAKES 20 ROLLS

1 pack of 20 frozen spring roll skins, defrosted if frozen

½ lb fresh bean sprouts

½ lb young tender leeks or scallions

¼ lb carrots

¼ lb white mushrooms

oil for deep frying

1½ tsp. salt

1 tsp. sugar

1 Tbsp. light soy sauce

● Wash and rinse the bean sprouts and drain thoroughly. Cut the leeks or scallions, carrots, and mushrooms into thin shreds. Heat 3–4 tablespoons oil in a wok or skillet and stir-fry all the vegetables for a few seconds. Add the salt, sugar, soy sauce, and continue stirring for about 1–1½ minutes. Remove and leave to cool a little.

● To cook the spring rolls, heat about 6 cups oil in a wok until it smokes. Reduce the heat for a few minutes to cool the oil a little before adding the spring rolls. Deep fry 6–8 at a time for 3–4 minutes or until golden and crispy. Increase the heat to high again before frying each batch. As each batch is cooked, remove and drain on paper towels. Serve hot immediately.

Sweet and Sour Vegetables

These vegetables have quite a strongly flavored sauce and should be served with plainer meats, fish, or poultry.

SERVES 4

1 Tbsp. olive oil

8 oz broccoli flowerets

½ red onion, thinly sliced

2 zucchini, sliced

1 carrot, cut into julienne strips

6 cups bean sprouts

1 cup mushrooms, sliced

2 Tbsp. honey

1 inch piece ginger root, shredded

2 Tbsp. light soy sauce

2 Tbsp. cider vinegar

114

● Heat the oil in a large skillet or wok and sauté the broccoli 3 minutes. Stir in the onion, zucchini, and carrot, and cook a further 2–3 minutes. Add the bean sprouts and mushrooms and cook 1 minute.

● Mix together the honey, ginger, soy sauce, and vinegar. Pour into the skillet, stir, and cook 2 minutes. Serve immediately.

Sweet and Sour Vegetables ▶

Spicy Beans

These beans have a rich caramel flavor due to the molasses and brown sugar. They are quite filling and almost a meal in themselves. Canned beans could be used for convenience.

SERVES 4

1⅓ cups dried beans, soaked overnight

1 tsp. salt

1 onion, halved and sliced

1 green bell pepper, cut into strips

½ cup diced cooked smoked ham

½ cup sliced spicy sausage

2 Tbsp. tomato paste

14 oz can chopped tomatoes

2 Tbsp. soft brown sugar

1 Tbsp. molasses

2 Tbsp. dark soy sauce

⅔ cup vegetable stock

1 Tbsp. cider vinegar

1 green chile, chopped

1 tsp. paprika pepper

● Drain the beans and rinse. Place the beans in a pan of water with the salt. Bring to a boil and boil rapidly 10 minutes. Remove any foam with a slotted spoon. Drain well.

● Heat the oven to 350°F. Place the beans in a casserole dish. Add the onion, pepper, ham, and sausage. Mix the tomato paste, tomatoes, brown sugar, molasses, soy sauce, stock, vinegar, chile, and paprika. Pour over the bean mix, stir, and cover. Cook in the oven, 50 minutes.

Potato Rosti

The recipe makes eight small rosti, but the mixture could be fried in a heavy-based skillet for one large rosti.

SERVES 4

3 Tbsp. vegetable oil

1 large onion, shredded

1 garlic clove, minced

1 Tbsp. light soy sauce

1½ lb potatoes, shredded

1½ cups shredded zucchini

¼ cup shredded Emmenthal cheese

salt and ground black pepper

● Heat 1 tablespoon of the oil in a large skillet and cook the onion, garlic, and soy sauce until the onions are softened, stirring occasionally, 5 minutes. Place the shredded potatoes in a bowl and add the zucchini and cheese. Season. Stir in the onion mixture.

● Using floured hands and a floured surface, shape the mixture into eight small round patties. Heat the remaining oil, in a skillet and fry the potato cakes in two batches on each side until golden, 5 minutes. Remove, drain on paper towels, and serve.

Mixed Bean Balls

These bean balls are great for kids or as a vegetable served with curries and stews. They can be threaded onto skewers for vegetarian kebabs.

SERVES 8

1⅓ cups mixed dried beans

1 Tbsp. olive oil

1 tsp. ground cumin

½ tsp. ground coriander

1 red onion, diced

2 garlic cloves, minced

1 green chile, diced

1 Tbsp. chopped fresh parsley

2 Tbsp. dark soy sauce

● Place the beans in a mixing bowl and cover with cold water. Cover and let soak overnight.

● Drain the beans and rinse under cold running water. Place the beans in a large pan, cover with fresh water, and bring to a boil. Boil rapidly 10 minutes. Lower the heat and simmer a further 50 minutes. Drain well and reserve.

● Heat the oil in a skillet and sauté the spices, onion, garlic, and chile 5 minutes. Place the contents of the skillet in a bowl and add the beans, fresh parsley, and soy sauce. Mash well. Roll the mixture into 24 balls and cook under the broiler, turning, 8 minutes. Serve hot.

Mushroom Pilaf

Mushroom pilaf is tasty enough to be served alone as a side dish. Or, it can be used as a base on which to serve stir-fried entrées.

SERVES 4

2 tsp. butter

1 cup mushrooms, sliced

½ cup chopped onions

1 garlic clove, minced

½ tsp. salt

1 cup wholewheat rice

1 cup rosé wine

1 cup chicken stock

1 Tbsp. light soy sauce

2 Tbsp. shredded Romano cheese

● Heat the butter in a pan and cook the mushrooms, onions, and garlic until soft but not browned. Add salt and rice and sauté about 5 minutes. Stir in the wine, chicken stock, and soy sauce.

● Cover and simmer until the rice is cooked, adding more liquid as necessary. When the rice is ready, stir in the cheese.

Deep-fried Mushrooms

Using different varieties of wild and cultivated mushrooms makes this dish very attractive. If possible, marinate the mushrooms for up to 5 hours for a really strong flavor.

SERVES 4

1 cup oyster mushrooms

1 cup shiitake mushrooms

1 cup open cap mushrooms, peeled and halved

⅔ cup red wine, such as burgundy

2 garlic cloves, minced

3 Tbsp. red wine vinegar

2 Tbsp. dark soy sauce

2 Tbsp. chopped fresh chives

¼ cup all-purpose flour

For the Batter

1 egg

⅔ cup water

1 cup all-purpose flour

1 Tbsp. shredded Parmesan cheese

● Place the mushrooms in a shallow dish. Mix together the wine, garlic, red wine vinegar, soy sauce, and chives. Pour over the mushrooms, cover, and marinate 2 hours.

● Beat the egg and water for the batter together. Sift the flour into a bowl and stir in the cheese. Make a well in the center and gradually beat in the egg mix to form a smooth batter. Heat the oil in a wok to 375°F.

● Remove the mushrooms from the marinade and roll in the flour. Dip into the batter to coat. Deep fry until golden, 3 minutes. Drain and pat dry with paper towels. Sprinkle with Parmesan cheese and serve.

Glazed Carrots

This a very quick recipe for glazed carrots which are often baked in the oven. Quite sweet to taste, they make a delicious accompaniment to roast meats.

SERVES 4

1 lb baby carrots

juice of 2 small oranges

2 Tbsp. butter

2 tsp. soft brown sugar

2 tsp. dark soy sauce

2 tsp. cornstarch

grated rind of 1 orange

1 Tbsp. chopped fresh chives

ground black pepper

● Cook the carrots in boiling water 6–7 minutes. Meanwhile, mix the orange juice, butter, sugar, soy sauce, orange rind, and chives in a pan.

● Blend the cornstarch with 4 teaspoons cold water and add to the pan. Bring to a boil, stirring until thickened. Drain the carrots. Place in a serving dish, pour over the sauce, and serve.

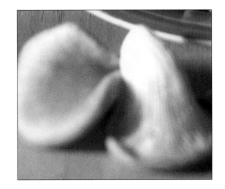

Sesame Bread Rolls

Make bread rolls deliciously different with the addition of soy sauce and sesame seeds. Serve warm to appreciate the flavors fully.

MAKES 20

1 lb strong white bread flour

2 tsp. salt

1 Tbsp. butter

2 packages active dry yeast

2 Tbsp. sesame seeds

2 Tbsp. light soy sauce

1¼ cups lukewarm water

milk for brushing

sesame seeds for topping

● Sift the flour and salt into a large mixing bowl. Rub in the butter to incorporate fully. Stir in the yeast and sesame seeds.

● Mix together the soy sauce and water and add to the dry ingredients. Bring the mixture together to form a smooth dough. Turn onto a lightly floured surface and knead for 10 minutes until smooth and elastic. Transfer to a lightly greased bowl, cover, and let rise 1 hour or until doubled in size.

● Turn onto a lightly floured surface and knead 5 minutes. Divide the dough into 20 equal sized pieces. Roll each piece into a sausage shape 6 inches in length and tie into a loose knot. Repeat with all the dough pieces. Place on a lightly greased baking sheet and let rise 30 minutes.

● Preheat the oven to 450°F. Brush the rolls with milk and sprinkle with sesame seeds. Bake in the oven until golden and the base sounds hollow when tapped, 15–20 minutes. Serve warm.

Steamed Mixed Vegetables

Steaming is one of the healthiest methods of cooking vegetables; they retain more of their nutrients than in boiling or baking. The colors also remain more vibrant, making these parcels a delight to open.

SERVES 4

1 cup cauliflower flowerets

½ cup snow peas

½ cup chestnut mushrooms, quartered

1 red onion, cut into 8 pieces

½ cup canned bamboo shoots, drained

¾ cup asparagus spears, trimmed

1 orange bell pepper, quartered and cut into thin strips

2 Tbsp. light soy sauce

1 tsp. fish sauce

1 tsp. dried lemon grass

4 tsp. lemon juice

2 tsp. fennel seeds

● Cut 4 large squares of baking paper. Divide the vegetables equally between the paper and scrunch the paper together to form a parcel.

● Mix the soy sauce, fish sauce, lemon grass, lemon juice, and fennel seeds. Spoon the mixture on top the vegetables and seal the parcels well. Cook in a steamer until the vegetables are tender, 20 minutes.

Zucchini and Sweet Potato Casserole

The colors of the zucchini and sweet potato make this very pleasing visually. The vegetables are baked in sour cream and topped with melting mozzarella cheese so taste delicious, too!

SERVES 4

1 lb sweet potato, sliced

1 lb zucchini, sliced

1 leek, sliced

1¼ cups sour cream

½ tsp. ground allspice

1 Tbsp. light soy sauce

1 Tbsp. fresh thyme

½ cup sliced Mozzarella cheese

salt and ground black pepper

● Cook the sweet potato, zucchini, and leek in a pan of boiling water 15 minutes. Drain well. Preheat the oven to 325°F. Arrange the zucchini and potato in a shallow ovenproof dish with the leek. Mix together the sour cream, allspice, soy sauce, and thyme. Season well. Pour over the vegetables.

● Arrange the cheese on top of the vegetables. Bake in the oven until golden, 30 minutes.

Lima Bean and Walnut Casserole

Lima beans and walnuts are a great combination, especially when cooked in a mustard sauce and topped with melting cheese.

SERVES 4

1 lb lima beans, shelled

2 Tbsp. butter

1 onion, cut into 16 pieces

1 garlic clove, minced

½ tsp. curry powder

5 Tbsp. vegetable stock

2 tsp. wholegrain mustard

2 Tbsp. light soy sauce

1 cup walnut pieces

½ cup shredded Cheddar cheese

salt and ground black pepper

● Heat the oven to 350°F. Cook the beans in boiling salted water 5 minutes. Drain well.

● Meanwhile, melt the butter in a skillet and cook the onion, garlic, and curry powder 5 minutes until softened. Stir in the stock, mustard, soy sauce, walnuts, seasoning, and drained beans.

● Transfer the mixture to a shallow ovenproof dish and sprinkle with cheese. Bake in the oven until the cheese has melted, 30 minutes. Serve at once

Lima Bean and Walnut Bake ▶

Index